BASIC SPIRITUAL WORKOUT

Be laed by y
God!

Bob
R. Ee

Basic Spiritual Workout

*A Guide to Christian Growth
for Catholic Youth*

BOB RICE

CHARIS

SERVANT PUBLICATIONS
ANN ARBOR, MICHIGAN

Charis books is an imprint of Servant Publications especially designed to serve Roman Catholics.

Servant Publications—Mission Statement
We are dedicated to publishing books that spread the gospel of Jesus Christ, help Christians to live in accordance with that gospel, promote renewal in the church, and bear witness to Christian unity.

Scripture verses are taken from The New Jerusalem Bible, copyright 1985, 1990 by Darton, Longman & Todd, Ltd. and Doubleday, a division of Bantum Doubleday Dell Publishing Group, Inc. Excerpts from the English translation of the Catechism of the Catholic Church for use in the United States of America Copyright 1994, United States Catholic Conference, Inc.-Libreria Editrice Vaticana. Used with permission.

Published by Servant Publications
P.O. Box 8617
Ann Arbor, Michigan 48107
www.servantpub.com

Cover design: Alan Furst Inc., Minneapolis, Minn.

03 04 05 06 10 9 8 7 6 5 4 3 2 1

Printed in the United States of America
ISBN 1-56955-360-2

Library of Congress Cataloging-in-Publication Data

Rice, Bob, 1972-
  Basic spiritual workout : a guide to Christian growth for Catholic
youth / Bob Rice.
     p. cm.
  ISBN 1-56955-360-2 (alk. paper)
  1. Catholic youth--Religious life. I. Title.
  BX2355.R53 2003
  248.8'3'08822--dc21

                                                                2003001270

*For Catholic youth who have committed themselves
to a deeper relationship with Jesus Christ*

Why Should I Read This Book?

Because you want *more*. And you're willing to work for it. Athletes know they need a good trainer if they are serious about winning. This book contains a wealth of information that our Catholic faith has handed down over the past two thousand years on how to be spiritually healthy and strong in Christ. In these pages you will discover how to experience God in new ways, intimately connect with him in prayer, learn how to be free from sin, and find out what it means to become part of the family of God.

But I'll be honest with you, it's not going to spoon-feed you like a baby. You're going to have to work for this if you want to make it real in your life. Do you want to be a saint? If it were easy, then everybody would be one. But here is what the church teaches about how to make that happen.

Contents

Prologue

I stood upon a mountaintop and looked at the stars. Growing up in a suburb of Chicago, I'd never seen the sky so clear or the galaxy so bright. I sat down on the Colorado soil. It was a warm summer night, but the ground felt cool to the touch. I breathed in and held that breath as if I were trying to capture time, as if I could pause that moment forever.

And as I breathed out, I said the word, "Yes."

I'm not sure if it was audible to man or creature, but I know it was to God. The proof of that is the very book you're reading.

When I was fifteen years old I went to a church camp in Colorado. It was there that somebody told me that Jesus Christ loved me. Now, it's not like I hadn't heard that before. I was raised in a Christian family: my mom was Catholic and my dad was Episcopalian. We went to church each Sunday, prayed before meals, and even talked about God as a family. My aunt was a Carmelite nun and my grandmother, who lived with us, was a strongly spiritual woman who prayed a rosary every day, I think. I frequently heard that Jesus loved me.

So why was that moment different?

Was it the way it was said?

Was it the way that I listened?

11

Maybe before, nobody had ever asked me to do anything about it. "Jesus loves me" was a statement of fact, not a statement of faith. It was a pleasant bit of information, like the sky being blue, or the sun keeping the earth in orbit. I was glad Jesus loved me, just as I was glad that a cold glass of water could refresh me on a hot summer's day. I prayed to Jesus every night, mostly thanking him for stuff and asking him for stuff. And if you had asked me if I loved Jesus, I would have answered yes. Because I did, as much as I knew. And if you had asked me if Jesus loved me, I would have answered yes, because he did. As much as I knew.

But that night I learned more. I heard about a God who came to earth, who walked among us, who died on a cross. I heard about a crucifixion, a resurrection, and an invitation. I saw the blood flow from his sacred head and sanctify the sinful ground. I heard about the devastating results of our sinfulness, and the incredible grace that was given by God.

After hearing that, the phrase "Jesus loves me" could never be the same. And I knew that my love for God could not be the same, either.

Because Jesus not only loved me, he *wanted* me. He wanted me to be a part of his life, a part of his plan. He wanted me to surrender myself to him, to be obedient to him, to follow him. He wanted this from me because he wanted the best for me. He made me, and wanted to complete the great work that he had begun in me. He knew the road to him was narrow but that it was the best. He knew that there was no true happiness or true freedom apart from him. And he reached out to me with his pierced hand and asked me if I would let him be my God.

And as I breathed out, I said the word, "Yes."

I hope that what brings you to this book is an experience such as the one I described. And if that is not the case, then I hope that reading this book will bring about such an experience in your life. If you are like me, you probably had (and have) many questions about God. The simple ones, the "who, what, where, when, why, and how" questions can be answered briefly here.

The "who" is Jesus.

The "what" is his calling for you.

The "where" is here.

The "when" is now.

The "why" is because he loves you.

And the "how"?

The "how" is what the rest of this book is about.

Read on.

ONE

Be Like Him

Growing up in Chicago in the 1980s and early '90s, there was one name that was synonymous with greatness:

Michael Jordan.

When he retired from the National Basketball Association after leading the Chicago Bulls to three consecutive championships, the city put a statue of him in Daley Plaza in downtown Chicago. Of course, I'm talking about the first time he retired. A year later he came back and led the Bulls to three more consecutive championships.

He had a great story. He was cut from his high school basketball team, but that only made him work harder. He was not the tallest or biggest person on the court, but he was the most determined to win. He inspired his teammates, intimidated his opponents, and excited his fans.

And everybody wanted to be like him. Stores couldn't keep jerseys with his number on it on the shelves. There was even a popular sports drink ad that showed people trying to do his moves with the phrase sung in the background, "I want to be like Mike."

One of the coolest things about him was that you felt like he earned the accolades he got. While some players base their talent on their physical attributes (like height, for example), with Jordan you felt like he worked hard for his success. And even more, you felt that just maybe, if you worked hard enough, you could be that way, too.

That's what made him different. He wasn't someone you just *admired*, he was someone who *inspired* you to be better than you were. You might chalk this up to the rambling of a Chicago native, for as time passes the mystique of Michael fades more and more into the distance. Of course, that is natural. People like that usually fade in popularity as time goes on.

Except, of course, for one person who actually became *more famous* after he died. I'm talking about Jesus.

Yes, there's a statue of Michael Jordan in downtown Chicago, but how many more statues are there of Jesus in the world? I think they named Jordan's high school gym after him, but how many buildings are dedicated to the name of Jesus Christ?

It's mind-boggling when you think of it. Jesus' life story, the Bible, has been printed in the billions. And people two thousand years later are still willing to give their life for him.

If you're still not convinced that we're talking about the greatest, most admired person in history (whether you're a Christian or not), just look at the calendar. The year is preceded by the initials *A.D.* That's an abbreviation for the Latin phrase *Anno Domini*, or "year of the Lord." After Jesus died, they *renamed time after him.* Now everything in human history is measured by how many years it happened before he was born (B.C.) or how many years after.

Michael Jordan was one of the most popular athletes of all time, but I don't think they'll rename time after him when he dies. And though many people wished they could "be like Mike," many more have given their lives to be like Jesus.

People who work out often have pictures on their wall of individuals who inspire them. A friend of mine (from Philadelphia) has Rocky posters in his basement where he lifts weights. Others have pictures of great athletes or muscular movie stars. When they hang those posters, what they're really saying is that they want to be like this person in some way. The picture inspires them to be more than they are right now. It reminds them why they are working so hard, and keeps them focused on the goals they are trying to achieve.

As followers of Christ, we have a goal: *to be like him.* This simple thought is actually the most crucial in your spiritual life. If you are going to get serious about being spiritually fit, then you need to know how to get fit and why you're doing what you're doing. People who don't think they're fat usually don't diet. People who don't think they're weak usually don't lift weights. Often it's when they come in contact with someone stronger, skinnier, or healthier than them that they start thinking about what kind of shape their body is in, and what they can do to make it better.

Most people think they are automatically going to heaven, as if there were no real effort involved in getting there. A lot of people say (and think) they love God, even if nothing in their personal or private life gives evidence of that statement. It's only when we come in contact with someone who is truly holy, someone who is passionate about their faith, someone who is radiant with the joy and love of God that we think, "What do they have that I don't have?" And we want to be like them.

I hope you have met people like that in your life. In fact, I bet most of you have if you're reading this book. It is usually the example of a relative, priest, friend, youth minister, musician, speaker, or whoever else turns a light on in our darkness that gives us this crazy thing called *hope.* And we think that maybe, with some effort, we can be that way, too.

My brother or sister, I want to introduce you to the Source. While other people can point to him, it is he who is the Way, the Truth, and the Life. He is the One we all want to be like. He is the reason why we want to run this race to the finish.

But here's the amazing thing: *Jesus is not just some figure in history.*

He is alive. He is active. And he is inviting you to be with him. He's not just a picture on the wall, but a person in your heart. Imagine a person you idolize, whether that be an athlete, artist, intellectual, or rock star. How incredible would it be if that person rang your doorbell and wanted to spend time with you?

That's what is happening, right now, with Jesus. He's knocking at your door, inviting you to share in his life. But if you really want to be like him, then you have to answer this one crucial question:

Who is he?

The Face of Love

God is not just a concept. It is, or I should say *he* is, a person. His name is Jesus. And he was a really cool guy who wore a long white robe and sandals. He walked around the land of Israel and told everybody to love each other. He was gentle and peaceful, like a shepherd quietly holding a sleeping lamb in his arms. Everybody liked him. And he was really, really nice.

Take for example, this passage of Scripture:

> *Jesus went up to Jerusalem, and in the Temple he found people selling cattle and sheep and doves, and the money changers sitting there. Making a whip out of cord, he drove them all out of the Temple, sheep and cattle as well, scattered the money changers' coins, knocked their tables over and said to the dove sellers, "Take all this out of here and stop using my Father's house as a market."*
>
> JOHN 2:13-16

What? Jesus with a whip? No, I'm sorry. That wasn't the Scripture I meant you to read. I was looking for something where he talked about loving each other, like this:

*Do you suppose I am here to bring peace on earth? No, I tell you ...
I have come to bring fire to the earth, and how I wish it were blazing already!*

LUKE 12:51, 49

OK. Clearly there is something wrong with this translation of the Bible I'm reading. What I meant to share was:

Two bandits were crucified with him ... and about the ninth hour, Jesus cried out in a loud voice ... "My God, my God, why have you forsaken me?"

MATTHEW 27:38, 46

"Why have you forsaken me?" What kind of talk is that? Shouldn't he be saying something like, "Don't worry everybody, I'll be back in three days!"

Hmm ... Maybe some of these stereotypes of Jesus don't really fit.

A few years back this country experienced "WWJD?" It was on bracelets and T-shirts and hats. Every church had a sermon on it, and every mall sold something with those initials on it. It stood for "What Would Jesus Do?" It became popular ... too popular.

It started with a group of devoted Christians who were trying to live the way Jesus lived. It ended as a fashion statement. People who weren't even Christians could be found wearing the WWJD bracelet.

Now, I'm not trying to be cynical. I think that anything that can get the message of Jesus Christ out to a large group of people is awesome. But I think there were many who got the wrong message. They equated "Be like Jesus" with "Be nice to everybody." They thought Jesus was a nice guy, a peaceful hippie who never condemned anybody and just wanted everyone to get along.

But think about it. Nice guys don't get crucified. He died a powerful death because he lived a powerful life. He challenged the authorities of the time. He hung out with prostitutes, and ate at the house of tax collectors (who were extortionists and traitors). He was radical. He was passionate. God was not a concept to him, he was a Father. Following him was not just a job, it was a way of life. He bent down to touch those who desired the truth; he stood firm against those who would live in lies.

We often choose our actions because we want to be loved. He did things because he *was* love. He came into this world not in riches, but in poverty. He grew as we did. He experienced the loss of his earthly father. He walked the earth. He knew what it was like to have no shade on a hot day, or to be weary at the end of one. He laughed with his friends. He cried when they died. He knew hunger. He knew pain. He died on a cross that he carried to his death. He saw his mother weep at his execution. The Letter to the Hebrews tells us that Jesus Christ was like us in all things but sin (see Heb 4:15). He was not a stereotype, a parable, or a fictional character.

He was as real as it gets.

The Second Person of the Trinity became flesh and dwelt among us so that we might know who God is. His name was **? Who Is Jesus?** Jesus, literally meaning "God saves." He was born over two thousand years ago, but he always was, always is, and always will be. He was the living Word that spoke to create the universe. He is, like the Father and the Holy Spirit, God. He rose from the dead, and now reigns in the heaven that he opened up for all his followers.

Oh, and one more thing. He's coming back.

You *will* meet him face-to-face. All people will, whether they believe in him or not. Many will reject this face of Love, as they did in the time he walked the earth. It will be their condemnation.

But you are responding to his call. The tears in his eyes will be tears of joy for a child who has finally made it home. At that moment of encounter, there will be so much to say, but only one thing is needed:

Jesus.

And he will love you forever.

To Know Him Is to Love Him

Our journey to "who Jesus is" begins with erasing stereotypes of who Jesus is not. He is not a wimp, not a boring teacher, not an angry judge. He's not out to ruin your fun, but his primary concern is not that you feel happy all the time, either. He is the most loving, dynamic, passionate, exciting, and dangerous person you will ever encounter.

Dangerous? Oh, yes. That's why they had him killed. He wants to uproot your way of life, have you do things that the world would consider insane. There are still many places in this world where even just to say you follow him would land you in jail. It is not safe to be a follower of Christ. Read the Bible ... it never has been.

So why are you so excited? Because following Jesus is the *real life*. It is, in his own words, "Life to the full" (Jn 10:10). This is something worth giving your life to. *O poor wandering soul, looking for the reason for existence. You have found it in him.*

But your journey has just begun. And it's a journey that only you can take. I'll be honest. I'll try to write as best I can, but that won't change a thing unless you are willing to work at this relationship with him. Clever phrases won't change your heart; encountering Jesus Christ will.

If you're reading this book, you've probably encountered him in some way already. Maybe you've read a bit of the Bible, or heard the gospel preached somewhere. You might have experienced him in a sacrament, or felt his presence in someone that you love (or someone who loves you). Even if you're reading this book "cold," you have just begun to meet him in what I have written about him.

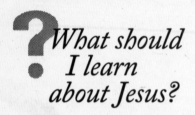

What should I learn about Jesus?

The goal is to get to know him, because that's when we can love him and feel his love for us. When you think about it, our ability to love is often based on our knowledge. I walk by two people at the grocery store. To one, I say "hello" because I know the person from work; to the other I say a quick "hi" but move on because we've never met before.

What is the difference between the two people? Is it that one is better than the other and therefore more deserving of my time? No, it's not about them. It's about *me*. I have more love for the one I know simply because we're already acquainted. It may very well be that if the stranger and I got to know each other, we might become best friends. But how would I know if I didn't introduce myself, or make an effort to get to know more about him?

I'm not advocating that we approach strangers at grocery stores and pour out our hearts. But what if that stranger came up to us? What if he helped us carry the groceries that were falling out of our hands? What if he paid for them because we ran out of money? Would our attitude be, "Thanks for the free food" but never ask his name, where he was from, and why he was doing this? Wouldn't the experience of knowing the giver be even greater than just experiencing the gift?

The questions answer themselves. Yet too often we focus more on what God can do for us than on who he is. If this is why you have come to him, then all I can say is ... welcome to the club. Our sin has caused so much destruction in our lives, that we are desperate for salvation. We need a doctor to bring us back to life. And to be honest, we've probably tried other "doctors" before that we thought would save us, but they only left us in a more miserable condition.

So finally we turn to God. He embraces us with his love. He heals us with his mercy. Yet too often I see people let that be the beginning and end of it. They come to a Mass or a retreat, feel the healing love of God, and then walk away as if they just popped in and out of an emergency room. And they miss the greatest thing. They miss the reason for life.

They miss knowing Jesus.

St. Paul remarked, "Because of the supreme advantage of knowing Christ Jesus my Lord, I count everything else as loss ... and look on them all as filth if only I can gain Christ" (Phil 3:8). He realized that the greatest thing on this journey wasn't learning about the sites he was seeing, but getting to know the tour guide. It's not only about liking the gift, it's about loving the giver. The greatest treasure he gives us is not just life, but life with him.

The journey begins by saying, "Who are you?" and to say that we must humbly admit that we do not know the answer. We must live our lives asking "What would Jesus do?" but we must not base our answer on our own opinions.

Knowing Jesus is an attainable goal, only because he wants to be known by us. What we know of God is what he told us himself. Our information isn't from a bunch of wise old guys spouting philosophy about who they think made the universe. God became man. Many people witnessed this and wrote about it for us. Many of those gave their lives defending the truth of what they said.

It is not safe to follow Jesus, but it is worth it. And it can be done. You can do it, because God will give you the grace to do it. You will stumble and fall. You will do great things and experience awesome blessings. You will be humbled and you will be lifted up. You will see the face of God and live.

The Commitment

But I have to make it clear that reading this book will not let you experience the love of God any more than watching an exercise video will help you get in shape. We are called to holiness, to live in the grace and life of Jesus Christ. *But nobody can be holy for you.* You can listen to the best talks, read the coolest books, and hang out with the holiest people but still not be in a loving relationship with God.

No, watching the video is not enough. You need to work out. And the idea behind the video is to help you establish your own routine so you can reach the goal of getting in shape.

That is what this book does. It's not a head-trip for intellectuals. It's not a temporary remedy to make you feel good. Relationships take a lot of work, and the good ones involve a life long commitment. There are three important things you'll need to make it on this journey:

1. *Be patient.* Nobody expects you to go into a gym for the first time and bench-press three hundred pounds. Even if you fail all the time, the love you have received is *unconditional.* Your sins will not stop God from loving you. St. Catherine of Siena once said, "Take God very seriously, and don't take yourself very seriously at all." Keep the

focus on God. When you fall, get up. And when you fall again, get up again. That is what the Christian life is all about. You have much to learn and it will take time. Pace yourself. You are running a marathon, not a sprint.

2. *Be humble.* *The Catechism of the Catholic Church* (which is a book written by the church that covers all its basic beliefs) tells us, "Humility is the foundation of prayer. Only when we acknowledge that 'We do not know how to pray as we ought,' are we ready to freely receive the gift of prayer" (CCC 2569). Being humble isn't about putting ourselves down all the time. Humility is truth: we realize that we are nothing in comparison with God. But humility also brings peace. Yes, we don't deserve his love, but he gives it to us anyway. This is the foundation of prayer because we realize that prayer is accepting an invitation, not demanding to be heard.

3. *Seek the face of Christ.* Scripture encourages us to "Keep our eyes fixed on Jesus, who leads us in our faith and brings it to perfection" (Heb 12:2). He is the goal, the reason why we run this race. He is the reason to be spiritually fit, so to speak. He is the only one who can love us and make us complete. He is the love of God.

Don't worry if your motivations seem selfish. You have a desperate need for what Jesus is offering you. In time, your "need" for his help will turn into a "want" for his heart. Be patient, be humble, and seek his holy face. Decide now to do whatever it takes to get to know him. Let's talk about the best way to do that.

What Should I Do Now?

There is a lot more to learn, but you can begin knowing Jesus right now by starting to read one of the four Gospels located in the New Testament of the Bible. They all tell the story of Jesus' life from the viewpoint of different people who knew him. Start reading half a chapter a day, and pray that the Holy Spirit will help you to not just *read* about, but *encounter* Jesus Christ.

TWO

Basic Nutrition

Do you want to "Get God?" Hear what Scripture has to say about experiencing the love of the Lord:

"*Taste* and *see* the goodness of the Lord" (see Ps 34:8).

"All those who *touched* him were saved" (Mk 6:56).

"If today you *hear* his voice, harden not your hearts" (see Ps 95:8).

"We are the *fragrance* of Christ" (2 Cor 2:15).

For many, God seems like an intellectual concept, a distant idea. But our God wants to be intimate with us. He is a God we can and should experience with our senses: taste, sight, touch, hearing, and smell. Those five senses that he gave us to experience his creation are the same ones he gave us so that we might experience him.

Before you drive the car, you have to put fuel in the tank. Before you can work out, you have to eat the right kind of food so that muscle can form in your body. Before you can persevere in the spiritual life, you have to "fuel up" through the various means the church gives us. But this is often where people make their first mistake when they begin their spiritual journey. They come off a retreat or a meeting feeling nourished by the presence of God. Their prayer time is wonderful, they are excited to be in love, and everything seems great. And then ... the experience ends. Prayer becomes dry, even tedious. They start at a sprint, drop to a run, then a walk, and then they stop. They get tired. They have no energy left for the journey.

Simply put, they run out of fuel.

Such a person will often long for the experience they had, wishing they could go back and tap into that energy they felt so strongly. But such things are rarely daily occurrences. However, God does offer us the fuel we need to stay strong in him, and we don't have to go to a conference with thousands of people to get it. It is present when we go to church, when we pray with friends, and when we open a Bible. You must actively seek this nourishment if you really want to be strong in your faith. Let us now, using the five senses, talk about ways you can be "fueled up" in Christ.

Taste

The central sacrament of our faith is the Eucharist. The word *Eucharist* literally means thanksgiving. We break bread in memorial of the death that Jesus died for us. But the sacrament is so much more than that.

Jesus Christ, the Second Person of the Trinity, the living Word of God, spoke the words "This is my body" and "This is my blood." This is the same voice that said, "Let there be light" and there was light. He needs to do nothing more than speak the words for things to become real. When he said "This is my body," the bread became his flesh. When he said "This is my blood," the wine became his blood. And when he turned to his apostles and said, "Do this in memory of me," they could. They could consecrate the bread and wine which then became the Body and Blood of Jesus Christ. The priesthood was formed and empowered by the living Word.

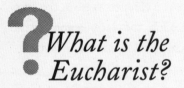
What is the Eucharist?

The Eucharist is the real presence, the Body and Blood of Jesus Christ. It is not a symbol, it is the real deal. Does it look like bread and wine? Yes, just as Jesus looked human but was more than that. He now humbles himself to give his presence to us in a way we can taste. We can physically receive him in his body, blood, soul, and divinity.

Why would he give himself to us in this great way? It is part of the incredible, joyful mystery of his love. It is why the Eucharist is called the "heart and the summit of the Church's life" (CCC 1407). As many grains of wheat are broken and united to make bread, so we too are broken and brought together to be transformed into the glory of God. As many grapes are crushed and aged to make wine, so we too must die and be brought back to life by the awesomeness of his mercy.

It was through *taste* that sin entered the world. The first sin was that of eating forbidden fruit. And it is through *taste* that sin is destroyed and eternal life is gained. Jesus said, "Anyone who does eat my flesh and drink my blood has eternal life" (Jn 6:54).

Let the Eucharist be your daily bread. It is your greatest source of spiritual nourishment if you receive it reverently and prayerfully. When you enter a church, look for the candle that burns by the tabernacle. That means Jesus is present there. Make the sign of the cross and genuflect toward it, being mindful of the One you are bowing to. Don't just go through the motions as if this were some empty ritual. You shouldn't be having conversations with others when you bow before God, nor should you be halfway into the pew. Take a moment to worship him there.

When you come to receive him, be mindful that you are not worthy, but you *are* invited. It is this invitation that allows you to receive his real presence. Do not fear, he wants you to receive him.

But do not take the host casually, popping it into your mouth as if it were some other kind of food.

The moments after you receive him are some of the most intimate moments you can have with God in this life. This is not the time to look at your watch and wonder when Mass will be over. Even when it ends, would it kill you to spend a few more minutes in prayer with him? Remember what you have received. He is the Bread of Life who can transform you forever, if you let him.

There are many who do not understand this great mystery. Don't be judgmental. Don't worry about anybody other than yourself right now. Pray for those who don't understand. And pray that you might understand more.

Scripture tells us to "taste and see that [the Lord] is good" (Ps 34:8). In the Eucharist, we can not only experience him through taste but also through sight. Eucharistic adoration is an awesome opportunity for prayer and worship, and happens at many churches every first Friday of the month, or occasionally throughout the year (these opportunities for Eucharistic adoration are also called Holy Hours).

And there are other ways to see him, too ...

Sight
Teenagers often hang large posters of actors, actresses, athletes, models, or rock stars on their bedroom walls. They do this because seeing the face of someone they admire makes them feel like they're in the person's presence.

We all love pictures. We put them in our wallets and hang them on our walls. I have a picture of my grandmother. She passed away a few years ago, but it comforts me to look at her photo because I feel like, in a way, she is still here with me.

In the same way, you should have pictures of Jesus to look at. Hang them in your room, place them in your wallet, stick them in your car, or put them in your school locker. It can be a drawing, a statue, a crucifix; it doesn't matter as long as it reminds you of the presence of Christ. Jesus came to be *seen*. He took on a human nature so that we might understand him better. Some Christian denominations avoid such practices, and think that Catholics worship pictures and statues. But we are just trying to experience God using all of our senses, and sight is one of the most powerful ones.

The best thing you can do with your sight is to read, and the best thing to read is the Bible. Don't let this statement be lost on you: **in your personal devotion, the Bible is the best way to encounter and learn about Jesus Christ.**

?Why should I read the Bible?

You probably have some negative stereotypes about the Bible, as you did about Jesus before you came to know him better. Many see the Bible as a nice collection of phrases and sayings that help you feel better about yourself and help you love everybody. That's not what the Bible is.

The Bible is a story. More than that, it's *our* story. And it is not for the faint of heart. It's a story of a God who would die for his people, and a people who often didn't want him. There's more sex, greed, and violence talked about in the Bible than in most movies. It's not a nice little fictional story, either. It's the truth, with all its ugliness and all its glory. The world has never seen anything else like the Bible.

Maybe that's why it's the most read piece of literature of all time and is a perennial bestseller. If this book were as lame and boring as some people make it out to be, would people still be reading it two thousand years later? Would it still be changing lives?

And that's the amazing thing about this book. St. Paul tells us that all Scripture is "God-breathed" (see 2 Tm 3:16). The Letter to the Hebrews says that the Bible is "living and active" (see Heb 4:12). We can encounter Christ when we open the pages of the Bible. The living Word has been written down so that we might continue to experience him in a personal way.

The words of the Bible are not just human words, but the *very words of God*. And we know how powerful his words can be. They create reality and make things happen. Through your Bible, you can come face-to-face with the living God. You can hear him speak to you. You can understand his heart. You can learn to be more like him. You can be transformed. You can be purified.

Fifteen years ago, someone told me to write a phrase on the inside of my Bible. It's still there: "This book will keep you from evil. Evil will keep you from this book." The Bible is one of your ultimate weapons to know God and to be protected from sin. You should read it, meditate upon it, and memorize it.

Yes, memorize it. Don't tell me you can't do it. How many of us can quote movies or song lyrics? Memorizing Scripture allows us to be continually in the presence of God. As Joshua (Moses' successor) once told his people:

"Have the book of the Law always on your lips; meditate on it day and night, so that you may carefully keep everything that is written in it. Then your undertakings will prosper, then you will have success" (Jos 1:8).

I know it's a big book, but you have a long life ahead of you. Where do you start? The answer is simple.

The Bible is broken into two parts: the Old Testament and the New Testament. The New Testament begins with four Gospels: Matthew, Mark, Luke, and John. These are four "pictures" of Jesus Christ. Begin your journey there. Get to know Jesus. He is the ultimate revelation of God for us, and all that we know of him is found in those four short books. They will take far less time to read than you think.

Have you ever been at a Mass where they decided to skip reading the Gospel? Of course not! It is central to our faith. It is *how* we know Jesus. There are other things in the Bible as well: stories of holy people and sinful people, poems about God's love, words of advice, teachings on the Christian life, and so on. You will get to those in time. You have enough to pray about in Matthew, Mark, Luke, and John. You can never "move on" from the Gospels because they are the foundation for the rest of what the Bible has to say.

So be a disciple of the Bible. Read it. Ask questions about it. Talk about it with your friends. Many people have died trying to get it into the hands of people whose governments have outlawed it. Many have died defending the truth of what it says. You hold in your hands the living Word of God, brought forth by the blood of martyrs. You hold the very words that can save souls from hell (including your own) and bring you closer to God.

You'd be a fool not to use it.

Touch

St. Paul wrote this: "From now onwards, then, we will not consider anyone by human standards: even if we were once familiar with Christ according to human standards, we do not know him in that way any longer" (2 Cor 5:16). Pay attention to his meaning there. We once thought Jesus was just a man. Now we know him to be more than that. In the same way, we once thought of each other as men and women from this family or that. Now we see that we are brothers and sisters in Christ, made in the image and likeness of God.

There are two aspects to this sense of touch that we must understand in order to be nourished by God's incredible love. The first is that we must let other people touch us. It is important to have a community of people who are walking this Christian life with you. I know you might not always like them, but they are your family and you need them (and they need you, too).

If you take a burning coal and put it amid a pile of rocks, what will happen? The rocks will warm for a bit, but eventually the coal will go out and the rocks will again cool. This is what happens to many who return from a religious event to their unsupportive friends. However, a coal placed among other burning coals burns a long, long time.

We need the touch of peers to keep us on fire in our journey. We need community to encourage us in a holy life. Not only do we need community, but we need to find good leaders who can teach us and pastor us in our walk with Christ. Beware of being unteachable! Don't think within a few months or years that you've "heard it all before" and no longer need to listen. We have all "heard it all before." Has there been a new piece of Scripture written in the last nineteen hundred years? Every time we hear it, we should let it sink deeper and deeper into our hearts so that we change into more righteous and holy people. And though the message may not change, we change each time we open our hearts to it.

You must have somebody to whom you can be accountable. It might be a group of people. But you can't hide in the darkness of your sinfulness. It will destroy you. Don't be afraid to talk about your struggles. Everybody has them. And there is nothing you can do to make God love you less.

Be careful in this endeavor. Put your trust in trustworthy people. I'd encourage you to stick to people of your own gender, and I wouldn't rely solely on somebody your own age. Pray for God to send people into your life who can encourage you into holiness.

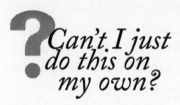
Can't I just do this on my own?

Jesus said an interesting thing. "Where two or three meet in my name, I am there among them" (Mt 18:20). Why would he say that? Does that mean that where one person is gathered in his name, he's not there? No, but he is making a point that he becomes present in community. We can experience his presence powerfully when many gather in his name.

He does not want Lone Rangers. He wants children who gather together and praise his name. I often see people who are uncomfortable with other people, and would rather pray by themselves. I was that way myself when I was growing up. But you must try to be a part of the group. I know it may be hard for you, and it may be the cross you have to bear for now, *but it is what God desires.* You don't get to choose who your brothers or sisters are, but it's up to you to make the family work.

Not only must we let ourselves be touched, we must go forth and touch others with the love of God. There was a town in Europe that the Nazis bombed during World War II. A large statue of Jesus stood in the center of the town. After the bombing stopped, the statue was shattered.

The townspeople were able to put the statue back together,

except one thing was missing: the hands. Someone made a sign and put it on the statue. It read:

"Christ has no hands now but yours."

This gift that you have been given is not meant for you to hold, it is meant for you to share. You are to be the hands of Christ, touching the world with his love. You can do this by serving Christ in the poor and needy, or proclaiming Christ to your friends.

God cannot be outdone in generosity. You can never "outgive" God. The more time you spend preaching his Word and serving his people, the more blessed and nourished by his presence you will be. You are like an extension cord. Your function is to be plugged into the wall (Christ) so that something can be plugged into you (others). That's when you find your true identity. You find yourself when you give yourself away.

St. Francis of Assisi told his followers: "Go and preach the gospel to all the nations. When necessary, use words." It is not eloquent speech that transforms hearts, but a joyful and holy life. Don't misunderstand the phrase: a time will come when words need to be spoken. But Jesus tells us, "Say whatever is given to you when the time comes, because it is not you who will be speaking; it is the Holy Spirit" (Mk 13:11).

Do not be passive in either of these endeavors. You must reach for fellowship and teachers just as you must reach for the needy, the lost, and the unloved. By doing this, God will expand your world and help you to be more and more in touch with him.

Hearing
Almost every description of heaven tells us that there is a lot of singing there: angels and saints constantly raising their voices to sing of the glory of God.

Music is powerful—so powerful that Saint Augustine said, "Singing is praying twice." How often have you had a tune stuck in your head? Or heard a song that changed your mood completely? Music that glorifies God can bring us into his presence, whether we are singing it ourselves, or just listening to it.

There is Christian music of every style and genre, and a lot of it is very good. You would do well to start listening to it, particularly music that focuses on praise and worship. If you fill your ears with songs that glorify God, you will be amazed at how much clearer your head will be.

But the most important thing you can hear is not music, but words. They are words spoken by a priest. He leans forward and tells you, "I absolve you of all your sins in the name of the Father, and of the Son, and of the Holy Spirit." I am talking about the sacrament of reconciliation.

? *Why should I go to Reconciliation?*

Before Jesus ascended into heaven, he breathed the Holy Spirit upon the apostles and said, "If you forgive anyone's sins, they are forgiven; if you retain anyone's sins, they are retained" (Jn 20:23). Now this is an incredible statement. Why didn't he just say, "Tell people that I will forgive them"?

In that moment, Jesus gave the apostles (the first priests) the authority to forgive sins in Jesus' name. Why did he do that? I would not dare to say I know the mind of God on this matter. But I can say this: Jesus wants to be personal with us. It is why he became man and dwelt among us. He desires one-on-one contact. He wants intimacy with us. And he comes to us in the sacraments.

God is present in the water that cleanses us in baptism. He is present in the oil that we are sealed with in confirmation. He is present in what was bread and wine in the sacrament of the Eucharist. And he is present in the words of absolution in the sacrament of reconciliation.

To absolve means to completely remove, to take away, leaving no trace. When the priest says, "I absolve you of all your sins," it is not the priest who is speaking. It will still sound like him, just as the Eucharist still tastes like bread and wine. But the voice speaking is actually the voice of Christ, the Word of God. And when the Word says something, it is done.

Reconciliation is there to forgive our sins and give us grace to overcome them the next time we face those temptations. Sometimes people ask, "Why do Catholics *have* to go to reconciliation?" My answer is always, "We don't just *have* to go, we *get* to go."

God gives us an incredible experience of grace in this sacrament. It heals us and strengthens us for the journey ahead. As Catholics, we are required to go at least once a year, but it is suggested that you go once a month. There's more on how to receive this sacrament in one of the "Bonus Sections" at the end of this book.

I know that reconciliation can be scary. If only we were as unwilling to do the sin as we were to confess it! But God desires that we hear his words of mercy so that we might know that we are not condemned, but saved by his love. And he wants his words to strengthen us in our battle against sin. Remember, his words create reality. What he says is what happens. And if he says that our sin is absolved, then it is. "If the Son sets you free, you will indeed be free" (Jn 8:36).

We are forgiven of all our sins. Is there anything that can be better to hear?

Smell

When the ancient Israelites presented sacrifices to God, they used incense. They would see the smoke rise to the heavens, and breathe in the fragrant offering they were burning. The incense they used had a special smell to it, set aside only for religious worship.

This tradition is carried on in our Catholic faith. Unfortunately, many churches don't use it much anymore, but the fragrant offering to God has always been a sign and symbol of our liturgies. And as Catholic Christians, the liturgy plays a central part in our faith.

The word "liturgy" means "public work of the people." The Mass we celebrate is not the priest's thing that we just watch. It is not a spectator sport. It is a community prayer in which we are to *actively participate*. That means we sing the songs, are attentive to the readings, give at the collection, and pray the prayers. We stand, sit, and kneel together to come into the presence of God and thank him for our lives. I know many who say, "I don't get anything out of Mass." Well, what do you put into it?

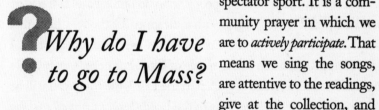
Why do I have to go to Mass?

Many of us are far too selfish when it comes to liturgy. We think it's there for us. It's not. We should come to Mass to worship God and bring him a sacrifice of praise. Is it hard to get out of bed some Sunday mornings? Of course it is. But it was also hard to die on a cross for our sins.

We go to liturgy, not for ourselves, but for him. That doesn't mean we don't get anything out of it. On the contrary, we are offered the Body and Blood of Jesus himself! As a Catholic, you need to go to Mass, at a minimum, every Sunday. If you can go during the week, you will be even more blessed. In the Mass you incorporate all the other senses as well: you taste of the Eucharist, you hear the music, the Word is read to you, you shake hands with your brothers and sisters in Christ. By doing this, you become, as Scripture says, "a fragrant offering to Christ."

Use Your Senses!

Receive the sacraments. Read Scripture. Gather with others. Share the faith. Go to Mass. These are all powerful ways in which Jesus Christ nourishes us. We need this nourishment if we are to stay strong with him and experience his love.

Our society has a word for people who do not have all five senses: handicapped. Do not become a handicapped Catholic. I have met people who have tasted the Eucharist but are blind to Scripture. I have seen people listen to the music of God, but never touch God's family. The more senses you open to the Lord, the more you will be able to experience his love. Pray to the Lord: *Jesus, I want all that you have for me ...*

What Should I Do Now?

Start using these ways to nourish yourself with Jesus. You should already be reading a bit of Scripture each day. Add to that some Christian music, or hang an image of Christ to remind you who it is that you are trying to get to know. If you have a faith community of some sort (like a youth group), commit yourself more to them. Start praying for those you'd like to share the gospel with. Most important, celebrate with all your "senses" at Mass, and go there to worship him.

THREE

Get Ready, Get Set ...

? *What is prayer?* In order to love someone, you have to communicate with them. Our communication with God is called *prayer*. Don't be intimidated by that word—the fact is that God created you for prayer. Cast from your mind whatever misconceptions you have about communicating with God. You don't need to be a hermit in a cave or a priest in a cathedral to pray to God. You can do it wherever you are, though some places are better than others.

Prayer is a lot like dance. There are many styles and many different forms. Some come naturally, others you'll have to learn. Like dance, the styles of prayer change when you are with a group of people and when you are by yourself. In my years in ministry, I have often found people who fall on either side of the spectrum: they love praying by themselves but can't stand group prayer, or they live for group worship and don't know what to do when they're alone with God.

Neither of these extremes is good. Usually, people like one way or the other because they are naturally disposed to expressing themselves either in a group or alone. What they often don't hear is that they need to *learn* how to pray in different ways.

We pray as individuals and we pray as a community. It's like walking with both feet. We need both personal and communal prayer to truly experience God in deeper ways. Our community encourages us and nourishes us. But we can't let that be the beginning and end of our spiritual life. Nobody can be holy for you, and you can't live out a relationship with God vicariously through someone else. You need time with him on your own.

To move ahead in prayer, you have to *learn* to pray. If you pray using only your natural ability, you will grow tired of it. It might be exciting at first, but eventually it will be like eating the same meal over and over again. You must *learn* to pray, and the church has two thousand years' experience in doing it.

A runner knows that the race is often won at the starting shot, before a step is even taken, by the runner who is most prepared and focused. If you're not ready and set before the race, you'll never win it. It's the same with prayer. You've got to prepare for it, by setting aside time and choosing a space. As the saying goes, "If you fail to plan, you're planning to fail."

Killing Time

When you wake up each morning, on the top of God's "To Do" list is that you use that day to draw closer to him. But on the top of the devil's "To Do" list is making sure the day becomes a distraction that lures you away from God's love.

Distraction is a good word for what Satan does. To distract is to draw attention away from something else. *Distraction* is the opposite of *attraction*, which means to be pulled towards. It is like the visiting player trying to make a free throw while the home crowd waves balloons and signs and makes noise, hoping that the player will miss the shot. Every professional basketball player learns to pay no attention to the chaos, but rather to focus on the basket. It is easier to allow ourselves to be *dis*tracted, so we must make a conscious effort to stay *a*ttracted to God. The way we do this is by sacrificing our time for prayer.

Let me speak to you in plain terms. To sacrifice means to kill. When the ancient Israelites sacrificed bulls and oxen, they would raise their swords and slaughter the beast. It was not an easy thing to do. These were big animals. Yet that was part of the reason why they sacrificed them. I mean, sacrificing a frog wouldn't take much effort at all. They killed not only one of the biggest animals they had, but also the one they valued the most, to show God that they put him before all other things in their lives.

? *What if I don't have time to pray?*

I know that your time is valuable, like the oxen our forefathers slaughtered. Yet you must sacrifice some of it in order to grow closer to God.

The most common excuse people give for why they don't pray is, "I don't have time." Did God give you fewer hours in the day than everyone else? What we are actually saying is, "I don't *make* time." And what our lives reflect when we don't make time is that other things are more important than God.

Yes, we have obligations in our lives. We go to school. We work. We are part of families and relationships. To spend time at these things is good—in fact it is what God calls us to do. But God also calls us to spend time with him, and we should make it a priority.

I have no illusions that this is easy to do. It's not. But you must. If you can't, the rest of this book will be completely worthless to you. Do not expect to "find" time for prayer, because the devil will hide that time from you. You must be willing to sacrifice some of the time you might spend on other things in your life: hobbies, activities, or sleep, for example. That doesn't mean you never do those things, it just means that you make prayer a higher priority.

However, you may find that you will need to give up some of the activities you do in order to really find God. I've known teens who have given up sports or other activities just to be more a part of their church. It was a hard decision for them, but I don't know any who have regretted it.

When Should You Pray?

Our communication with God can, and should, happen all the time. However, make sure to set aside a specific time of intimacy with God every day. This is the "workout" we are talking about.

It is a good discipline, when you are beginning your walk with Christ, to have a set time to pray each day. If you can't always do it the exact same time, then at least do it the same length of time. When you wake up in the morning (and say hello to God), ask his help to determine at that moment when your fifteen minutes will be. 3 P.M. to 3:15 P.M.? 6:15 A.M. to 6:30 A.M.? Treat it like you're making an appointment with God.

Here's something I would not suggest: doing it at the end of the day, only after you've done everything else. But even saying, "I'll do it at 11 P.M." is better than saying, "I'll do it whenever I'm finished with stuff." Be careful about postponing your intimate prayer into the evening hours. The later it is in the day, the more opportunities the devil will have to distract you from prayer.

This is probably why Scripture tells us the best time to pray is early in the morning. When you pray in the morning, you can offer up the entire day to him much more easily. You receive strength to face the day, and are ready for any challenges or opportunities that come.

I'm not a morning person, so embracing that discipline has been difficult for me. But it is true. And I've never lived a day when I've thought, "If only I had twenty minutes more of sleep" (if I'm in that state, I'm usually wishing for a few more hours). But I have mourned days without prayer.

Sacred Space

In our society, we designate certain spaces for certain functions. Take a house for example. We sleep in the bedroom. We make food in the kitchen. We wash in the bathroom. We hang out in the family room. Each space has a purpose.

Sometimes we might sleep in the family room or eat in the bedroom, but for the most part we are creatures of habit, and where we are directly connects to what we do. We do this outside our homes as well. We have structures where we study and learn (schools), places where we buy things (stores), and buildings where we worship and pray (churches). In fact, even in those churches, many have a specific seat they feel most comfortable in for worship!

Where we are connects to what we do. I know teens who tell me they fall asleep while they try to pray. The most common reason for this is that they pray while lying in their bed. It's no wonder they fall asleep!

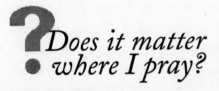
Does it matter where I pray?

When you physically work out, it's important that you prepare the space to do so: for example, you move the table out of the way or put down a mat. In a similar way, you must make a space for prayer. Most of us don't have the luxury of designating a separate room for it, but we can set aside parts of a room as sacred space.

You'll have to use some creativity, but here are three essential elements of your sacred space:

1. Visual: More than any other sense, the sense of sight conveys the most information to us about our world. Since sight is so immediate, it is good to have pictures or statues to focus on while you pray. A picture of Jesus, a cross, a picture of a saint, a statue of Mary ... these will all help keep your mind on God. These are natural reminders of the supernatural reality that God is with us. They aid us in our *distracted* weakness so we can be more *attracted* to God. Any object made and used with this intent is holy, but remember you're not worshipping the creation but the Creator. A Bible is a must for this space, and you might also include a blessed candle, rosary beads, or other items that draw you nearer to God. One of my friends kept three nails on her desk to remind her of the victory Christ won for her. Again, you can use some creativity here, but the point is that the space has a special look to it, so as your eyes start to wander they focus upon things that point your attention to God.

2. Practical: In design, people talk about *form and function*. Form is what something looks like, and function is what it does. You could have the nicest looking space, but it might not be practical for prayer. Your space needs to include an area for your Bible, or catechism, or whatever else you might be reading. It should be somewhat comfortable to encourage you to spend more time there. It should allow you to take different positions such as sitting, kneeling, and standing (this is a workout, after all). Most important, it needs to be located where you can be free of distraction but at the same time see and be reminded of God's presence.

3. Special: Wherever your space ends up and however it looks, make it a special place by using it (as best you can) *only* for God. I'm a bit of a messy person, but when I was in high school I set aside a third of a desk I had in my bedroom for Christ. I had a cross, a candle, and a Bible on it. My desk would be a total shambles with papers and schoolbooks everywhere——except on that third of my desk with my cross, candle, and Bible. I was continually tempted to put something there (particularly when the mess would get really out of control), but I knew if I did that I'd probably never get it back. The devil will try hard to destroy any space you put aside for God, because he knows how helpful that space is in your battle for holiness. Keep it special, and set aside only for him.

Those are just guidelines. It all depends on where you live, how you live, and with whom you live. One friend of mine had a whole wall with pictures and icons. Another teen I knew shared a room with two other people, so he had a portable sacred space that consisted of a cross and a picture of the Sacred Heart that he set up with his Bible when he'd pray and put away when he finished. Do the best you can, and ask God to help you to determine where it should be and what it should look like.

Such a space will really help you in your spiritual workout, but you mustn't become so dependent on it that you can't pray unless you are there. You can pray anywhere—at school, say, or in the car, or wherever you are during vacation. But you who are making a commitment to Christ should commit some portion of physical space to help you worship him. At the very least, it's a great witness to your love for him. A person seeing it might ask, "What is that for?" and it becomes a great opportunity to talk about your faith.

Once you've figured out where and when to pray, you're workout is ready to begin.

What Should I Do Now?

Clear out fifteen minutes of time for prayer, and make a space for it. The next chapter will give you more information on how to use that time, but it won't do you any good if you don't know when or where you're going to have your regular prayer time each day. For now, use the time to read Scripture and be nourished by his Word. You're going to need all the nourishment you can get for the workout that's ahead of you!

FOUR

Spiritual Workout

Timothy was a young man, and a follower of Paul. Apparently, Tim was in good shape, which is probably why St. Paul used the analogy of working out to help him understand how to approach his spiritual life. He wrote to him:

"Train yourself for religion. Physical exercise is useful enough, but the usefulness of religion is unlimited, since it holds out promise both for life here and now and for the life to come; that is a saying that you can rely on and nobody should doubt it" (1 Tm 4:7-9).

In physical training, there are different kinds of exercise to help the body in different ways. Cardiovascular exercises are aimed at improving blood circulation and making your heart grow stronger. Some exercises are primarily for burning fat and losing weight. Others are designed to increase muscle strength. Through all of them, it is important to stretch so that you don't injure yourself, and you must continue to breathe to have the strength to make it to the end.

All of these types of exercise relate to each other. For example, if you're doing aerobic exercises, you're sure to burn some fat and gain some muscle tone. But we make the distinctions so that a person knows the important elements to focus on when they work out, so that they can be in the best shape possible.

The same is true when we pray. Our church has celebrated two thousand years of Christian prayer, and teaches five different elements of prayer. Like a physical workout, these all relate to each other, yet it is helpful to make distinctions so we can be sure to truly grow strong with Christ. The five elements are:

- Blessing and Adoration
- Petition
- Intercession
- Thanksgiving
- Praise

Let's see how each of these can strengthen the spiritual body.

Cardiovascular (Prayer of Blessing and Adoration)

The heart is one of the most important organs. Located in the center of the body, it circulates blood through the lungs to refresh it and then sends it to the rest of the organs so that the body can function. The heart draws in blood from the body, and also pushes blood out. And blood is our life.

When we talk about the prayer of blessing, we talk about how we encounter God in prayer. Our prayer rises up in the Holy Spirit through Christ to the Father, and then God's grace descends from the Father through Christ in the Holy Spirit. Our Catechism states, "The prayer of blessing is man's response to God's gifts: because God blesses, the human heart can in return bless the One who is the source of every blessing" (CCC 2626).

The prayer of blessing is a dialogue of grace. God speaks the first word, but we must respond to keep the conversation going. God blesses us, and we bless God.

We bless God? Yep. We say things like, "Blessed be God forever!" or "Blessed be the Lord!" Well, who do we think is doing the blessing? Are we asking God to bless himself?

To bless means *to show favor to* and *to say "yes" to*. To bless something means to accept it as a good thing, and affirm it in our lives. God has accepted us in his life, and so we respond by accepting him. This is how prayer begins.

Clearly, we are not talking about an even exchange. The miracle here is not that the creation acknowledges the Creator as good, but that the Creator would care so much for the creature. As we stand in awe of his love for us, it leads us into *adoration*. Adoration is our awareness of God's incredible power and mercy. When we adore, we recognize that we are not just casually talking to another person, we are in conversation with the King of Kings and the Lord of Lords, who invites us into his divine life even though we are completely unworthy of it.

Blessing and adoration are therefore intrinsically connected. If blessing describes our encounter with God, then adoration explains how our attitude should be in that encounter. Both are founded on the primary virtue of prayer: *humility*.

We begin prayer by realizing the blessings of God and accepting the goodness of God in our lives (he blesses us and we bless him), and because of this we humbly bring ourselves into his awesome presence (adoration). There is no other way to begin prayer than with a "yes" to him and an acknowledgment of his greatness.

So now you're wondering, how do I do that? Well, it is the hardest and the simplest thing to do. It happens in the heart, not so much with words or sayings. In fact, the depth of this kind of prayer is often felt best in silence. It is like experiencing something awesome, like Niagara Falls or the Rocky Mountains. You stand before something so incredible, it takes your breath away and you don't know what to say. It's simple because it's just taking a moment to be real in front of God. It's hard because we're not used to doing that.

We live in a world where we are taught to act tough and wear masks. We suck in our gut and never admit our weaknesses. To stand honestly before God with our beauty and ugliness and acknowledge his love and gifts for us is ... well, humbling. We're often happy to give God the things we think are our strengths, but our weaknesses? Our sinfulness?

But if we don't start this way, we'll never truly encounter Jesus Christ in prayer. God is not interested in sitting through the act we put on for everyone else. He sees right through it. And you know what? He loves us anyway. There is great freedom in learning to be real before God, and it helps us learn to be real in front of everyone else. It is this attitude of humility, this acknowledgment of his greatness, and this acceptance of him in our lives that is what the prayer of blessing and adoration is all about.

Fat-burning (Prayer of Petition)

Not all fat is bad. I say this to a country often obsessed with weight. As Americans, we struggle with obesity almost as much as other countries struggle with starvation. In many other places in the world, the only eating disorders people have are lack of food, lack of clean water, and lack of nutrition.

In fact, our obsession with exercise may be a direct result of our obsession with eating. We think it's easier for us to run an extra mile than to avoid the fatty foods we like so much. We forget that even if we burn off the calories right away, the damage is done through the high amounts of cholesterol, caffeine, sodium, or other things that are in the meals or snacks we eat.

So what is fat? Learning about this in the physical world can help us understand how it relates to our spiritual lives. When we eat, our body takes whatever nutrients it needs (or are available) out of the food and turns the rest to fat. Fat gives us energy: we burn it off in daily activity, like a car burns fuel to keep going.

Simply put, fat is something our body gives us so that we can, in our various activities, give it away. It is meant to be a healthy part of our lives. Unfortunately, when we eat too much food or eat foods that are bad for us, this fat that gives us energy can have the opposite effect. It slows us down, we gain weight, our heart works overtime to keep blood flowing to our fatter body, and so on. What is worse is that the more fat a person gains, the harder it is to take it off.

Fat is like what theologians call our free will. God gave us the gift of free will at our creation. It was given so that we could be free to love God, but instead we used it to choose evil. And the more we chose against God, the harder it became to turn toward him. This is why Jesus died on the cross for us. He set us free from the cycle of sin that made us unable to reach him.

The prayer of petition is about burning off spiritual fat, both healthy and unhealthy. There are three types of prayers that are part of what the Church calls petition. We begin by burning off the fat that we got by overeating or by eating the wrong kinds of food. What I am talking about is *sin*. This first kind of prayer of petition asks forgiveness for ways that we have hurt God and others; we ask mercy for the ways that we have abused the freedom God gave us, the ways we have been selfish rather than giving.

? *How do I know if I've sinned?*   To do this, we must take a moment to look over our actions and compare them to the way God calls us to live. This is called an *examination of conscience*, and we need to do it if we are to receive God's grace in our lives. We so often justify the sin we do. We know we are not supposed to lie, but "I don't want to get in trouble and who would it hurt anyway?" We know we aren't supposed to have sex, but "I really care for this person and it's not like we're going all the way." We compare ourselves to others and think, "At least I'm not as bad as they are."

We feel guilty when we do wrong things, so we get around it by convincing ourselves that what is wrong is right. And just like fat, the more evil we absorb, the harder it is to get rid of it.

Jesus is offering to take this from us, but we must be able to name what it is we need to give him. This might mean that we realize there is more sin in our lives than we would like to admit. This would be overwhelming if it weren't for the power of the cross. There is no sin that is too big for him to forgive.

In order to understand if we have sinned against God, we must first know how God calls us to live. There is an examination of conscience in the Bonus Workout Material at the back of this book that takes the Ten Commandments and applies them to some modern-day situations (it's called Spiritual Checkup). This isn't meant to be an exercise in guilt, but an acceptance of God's mercy. Understanding our sin gives us freedom to turn away from it (only by God's grace) and live the fullness of life that only Jesus can give.

The other kind of fat we burn is the healthy kind, the kind that we were meant to burn off to give us energy. God has given us our free will, now we give it back to him. In the second prayer of petition, we ask that God's kingdom would come, and that his will would be done in our lives. Sound familiar? That's what Jesus taught us to pray in the Our Father. This prayer gives us the energy we need to live lives for God, rather than just for ourselves.

Some people assume that God's will is always done. This is why they are so confused when bad things happen in the world. If God's will were always done, then why would Jesus ask us to pray that it would happen? Free will means that he does not force himself on us, but respects our decision. He will work as much as we let him. And we must *ask* him to be active in our lives.

This leads us to the third and final prayer of petition. After we ask for forgiveness and pray for his kingdom, we then ask for our own needs. The order of these three things is important. Some people think prayer is just asking for stuff, like writing a letter to Santa. They are missing the point.

We pray for *his* will before *our* will and by doing this submit all our desires to him. This is the way God has told us to pray. Petitions done like this will never be selfish, because everything we ask for is about accomplishing his will. Remember, we have a big God. So don't be afraid to ask him for big things in your life. He *wants* to bless you. Let him.

So there are three kinds of prayers of petition, all of which will free us from spiritual fat: we repent of our sins, we pray for his kingdom and his will, and we pray for our needs.

Muscle-toning (Prayer of Intercession)
I think it's something we take for granted: the more we lift heavy objects, the stronger we become to lift them. Amazing, isn't it?

Many things in creation *weaken* with added weight. A table with three hundred pounds of weight on it is not as stable as one with one hundred pounds on it. And the more you put that weight on it, the more it will deteriorate over time. What do we have that doesn't weaken?

Muscle.

Though some people are physically larger than others, what really matters is not the height or weight, but the muscular strength. A five foot tall man can beat up a seven foot tall man if he's got more muscle. It's an obvious statement, but something we often overlook. For in nature, a seven foot rock is stronger than a five foot one, assuming of course that they are made of the same material and have the other two same dimensions.

Many seek to increase muscle in their body so that they can become more powerful. They see their physical strength as a means to get things done. Whether their use of this power is good or bad is not the topic right now. The point is that the stronger you are, the more you can make things happen.

This is the same in our spiritual life, except the power we seek is not for ourselves, but for others by the grace of God. The third form of prayer is the prayer of intercession. Whereas prayers of petition were mostly focused on self (*I* am sorry, *I* invite your will to be done, *I* need you), prayers of intercession are when we lift up intentions for others, even our enemies.

We lift weights to grow in muscular strength, but we lift up prayers for others so that we can grow in spiritual strength. Our Catechism states beautifully that our prayers of intercession are a "characteristic of a heart attuned to God's mercy" (CCC 2635). We reach out in prayer to the world around us that is so desperately in need of God.

The key to effective intercessory prayer is the same as the key to effective weight lifting: *repetition*. The more prayerful we become *about* the world, the more prayerful we will be *in* the world. St. Ambrose had a great quote on prayer: "Pray as though everything depended on God, and act as though everything depended on you." He understood that the real power is God's power, and we humbly beg for it in prayer.

For whom should we pray? Everybody. Even those who hate us. And I'm not talking about a selfish prayer, like, "Lord, teach that jerk a lesson." That's not praying for *them*, that's praying for *you*. A real prayer is, "Show that person your love and bless his day." Do you find that hard to pray?

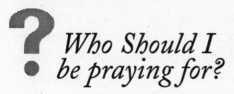

Who Should I be praying for?

Is it an intention that seems too hard to lift up? Praise God, because we need heavy things to lift in order to build muscle. How else do you expect to grow strong?

This is a good time to forgive others, too. And that can be the hardest prayer of all. To pray blessings on your enemies is not only to forgive them but to wish them well. Jesus knows how hard it is to forgive; he had to endure the cross to forgive us. The fact that we didn't *deserve* to be forgiven helps us to forgive those who have hurt us. (When you think about it, nobody ever deserves to be forgiven. That's what forgiveness is all about.)

Ask the Spirit to help you discern who and what to pray for. I know some who start with a short list, and in a few days have a longer list, then it grows to an incredibly long list. A few days later they give up and start saying, "God bless everybody. Amen." I refer to that as *pulling a spiritual muscle.* They strain themselves and just can't seem to do it anymore.

What's wrong with saying "God bless everybody"? I'd never say it's wrong, as if it were bad. But if that is the extent of your intercessory prayer, then you'll miss the great joy of seeing your specific prayers answered in other people's lives. You'll also be denying the desires of your heart that compel you to specifically reach out to those you feel called to.

Don't misunderstand: your prayers should include intentions for the world, the country, the church, and schools. But you should also pray for your neighbor who is struggling with cancer, your friend who has questions about the faith, your sister who is bothering you, and the sad person you passed on the way home. After you get through your general intercessions (world, country, school, church, and so on), take some moments of silence to see what the Holy Spirit would like you to pray for. God will bring people to your mind, whether friends or strangers. You should always pray for your family and for priests.

I'd encourage you to keep a list. Some of those items may stay there for awhile, but you'll be amazed at how many things you'll cross off. Scripture often encourages us to pray for each other, and that's what we do in the prayer of intercession. It's like muscle toning except in one crucial aspect. The muscle builder will face a heavy weight with self-confidence, thinking, "I can do this. I can lift this weight." The spiritual person faces the heavy problems of the world with surrender, thinking, "I can't do this. But Lord, I know you can, so please do."

Stretch (Prayer of Thanksgiving)

You have just worked your spiritual muscles in the prayer of intercession. It's time to stretch them out with prayers of thanksgiving. We take so much for granted! What do we have that hasn't been given to us?

Our life itself is a gift. No one can take credit for their own creation. Our prayers of thanksgiving should never lose sight of the obvious. When was the last time you thanked God for the ability to see? The ability to think? Let us not have to suffer tragedy in order to appreciate what we have. In my life I have experienced that people who have less are usually more thankful than people who have more. Those who have next to nothing are very aware and thankful that they have something. Those who have a lot are usually wondering (and whining) why they can't have everything.

What do I have to be thankful for?

Praying the prayer of thanksgiving is simple. In humility (the foundation of all prayer) we recognize that everything is a gift, and therefore give thanks for everything. That even includes difficulties through which God gives us opportunities to suffer as he did and draw closer to him. Clearly, we are not talking about being thankful for acts of sin, which are not of God. But we should be thankful for how God can work even in the face of great evil. Much has been said of the three thousand lives lost on September 11th when the World Trade Center collapsed. But people rarely focus on the estimated twenty-five thousand who escaped from those buildings, many with miraculous stories.

We have reasons to be thankful all around us, and in our spiritual workout it's important that we don't take things for granted. Like the prayer of intercession, this could turn into a very long list, and we could give up by saying, "God, thanks for everything. Amen." You should pray generally and specifically as the Spirit inspires your heart. Most important, always give thanks for answered prayer. It provides soothing relief to those muscles you worked so hard while interceding for others.

The *how* of thanksgiving is simple, but I'd like to take a moment to focus on *why* we should do it. Thanksgiving in prayer, like stretching in working out, is often overlooked. Yet it is crucial for success. Here are four results of this kind of prayer.

Increased Ability. Stretching actually increases the length of our muscles and tendons. That means they are able to do more for us. Stretching our body allows all the parts of our body to be more successful at what it wants to do. Blood flows better, which helps the heart. Muscles work more smoothly, which helps tone them and strengthen them. And it allows us to work harder and longer, which is imperative if we want to burn off fat.

When St. Paul wrote of prayer, he said this: "Never worry about anything; but tell God all your desires of every kind in prayer and petition shot through with gratitude, and the peace of God which is beyond our understanding will guard your hearts and your thoughts in Christ Jesus" (Phil 4:6-7). I love that phrase, "shot through with gratitude." It's like thanksgiving is the gunpowder that propels the bullet. Thanksgiving strengthens all aspects of our prayer, and makes it more effective. After all, how can we ask anything of God if we are not thankful for what we have? And aren't we more inclined to bestow favors on thankful friends than on those who are ungrateful? Our prayer of thanksgiving strengthens every aspect of all of our prayers.

Flexibility. Stretching makes our body more flexible. Thanksgiving does the same with our soul. When we get used to giving thanks in everything, we get used to seeing God work even when things look bad. Instead of rigid expectations of perfection, we become more flexible with life, recognizing God's work in all situations. This is "the peace of God which is beyond our understanding" that Paul was writing about. Stretching keeps the muscles relaxed so the body doesn't strain or injure itself during strenuous activity. Thanksgiving brings peace to our soul, so that we can continue to function properly even in difficult circumstances.

Endurance. Trainers say that many injuries occur because of muscle fatigue, and that stretching can rejuvenate those muscles and keep them from injury. Simply put, the better you stretch, the longer your muscles can last.

Again, we hear from St. Paul: "Be persevering in your prayers and be thankful as you stay awake to pray" (Eph 6:8). Gratitude leads to endurance. Have you noticed that when you are thankful to someone, you find extra energy to go out of your way to help that person? Thankfulness is a powerful motivation for prayer, and the more thankful we become, the more we are inclined to persevere in our spiritual lives.

Success. Veteran athletes know the importance of stretching the body. By increasing their body's ability, flexibility, and endurance, they are able to avoid injury and be more successful at what they do.

St. Paul writes, "Let your behavior be free of murmuring and complaining so that you remain faultless and pure, unspoilt children of God surrounded by a deceitful and underhand brood, shining out among them like bright stars in the world" (Phil 2:14-15). The opposite of "murmuring and complaining" is to be thankful. Jesus calls us to be "light for the world" (Mt 5:14). When we are thankful, we *shine*.

Thankfulness is more than making a list, it is an attitude of the heart. The Catechism goes so far as to say that, "Thanksgiving characterizes the prayer of the Church" (CCC 2637). As we have seen, the word "Eucharist" comes from the Greek word "to give thanks." If I have spent more time on this than other forms of prayer, it is only because our current culture is so *ungrateful*. It is cynical, sarcastic, and pessimistic. It often causes us to focus more on what we do not have than what we do have. Instead of trying to please God, this attitude makes us wonder why God isn't doing more to please us.

We are all affected by these attitudes. But don't worry. The cure for this spiritual "cramping" is as simple as stretching out your hands and saying with your heart, "Thank you, Jesus."

Do this all the time, every day. You'll not only find his peace, but you will also become his light for the world.

Breathing (Prayer of Praise)

It was a statement I used to mock: "Don't forget to breathe." Every trainer says it over and over again while guiding people in exercises. I'd laugh every time I heard them say it. Forget to breathe? *What idiot would forget to breathe?*

And then I started exercising. Sure enough, I found I needed that reminder. When we physically exert ourselves, we often subconsciously hold our breath. A person who bends down to pick up a heavy load instinctively takes a deep breath and holds it while lifting. For some reason, we think it strengthens us.

In part, it is true. The deep breath in our lungs brings oxygen to our blood and gives us a kind of energy rush. We want to keep this rush, so we hold in our breath. And that's where we make our mistake. Our lungs pull the oxygen out of the air and convert it to carbon dioxide. But now our lungs are filled, not with the life-giving oxygen our body needs to perform the activity, but with carbon dioxide that it wants to expel. Holding that breath turns our high into a low, and we can get light-headed, weak, and even collapse.

And so the trainers tell us, "Don't forget to breathe." When they say this, what they really mean is *don't forget to exhale.* Inhaling is not the problem. The problem comes when we try to hold the breath too long, and it turns from something life-giving into a liability.

The prayer of praise is like breathing. It is a fundamental part of our life. Whereas the prayer of thanksgiving focuses on what he has done for us, the prayer of praise is focused on who he is. There is a big difference.

? *What is the difference between praising God and thanking him?*

It is because he loves us for who we are, certainly not for what we do, that we can love him and others in the same way. Scripture tells us, "It is proof of God's own love for us, that Christ died for us while we were still sinners" (Rom 5:8). When we were at our worst, he was at his best!

In the face of such love, our first response is that of *thanks.* But if our thanksgiving is truly sincere, it leads us into a relationship with the One who gives. Yes, we come to him because of what he did for us, but we stay because of who he is. That is when we begin to *praise.*

The Catechism tells us that "praise embraces the other forms of prayer and carries them toward him who is its source and goal" (CCC 2639). It's like breathing. It's part of everything we do, if we're doing it correctly. When we bless God, we praise him. When we thank God, we praise him. When we confess our sin, we praise him. Praise is that aspect of our prayer that not only says, "Thank you, Lord," but "I love you, Jesus."

Though praise is blended in all of our forms of prayer, it also stands on its own. An athlete at the end of a strenuous workout will stand for a moment and breathe heavily. It's the natural reaction to physical exertion. So also in our spiritual life, if we are truly working to go deeper in our relationship with him, praise comes naturally. It's a reflection of how much effort we are putting into our prayers. If you saw someone at the end of a physical exercise who wasn't breathing heavily, you'd question how hard that person worked!

It's not complicated. You were born to do it. Take time to do it better. People who practice breathing increase their lung capacity. People who practice praise increase their love capacity. People who don't learn to breathe properly often get dizzy and black out. People who don't praise often get spiritually confused and lose sight of the One they are trying to be like. The prayer of praise is when we take time to tell him how wonderful he is. We don't "hold our breath." We naturally respond to the amazing and incredible God, who is "the Alpha and the Omega, the First and the Last, the Beginning and the End" (Rv 22:13). It's as simple as breathing out.

We just need to remember to do it.

Putting It Into Practice

Knowing how to work out doesn't make you fit. You've got to *do it*.

Here's what I, your spiritual trainer, want you to do. Spend at least fifteen minutes a day doing this workout. That's a little more than 1 percent of your day. I want you to break this down into three minutes per section. So take three minutes to bless and adore, three minutes for petition, three minutes for intercession, three minutes for thanksgiving, and three minutes for praise.

You need to build what I call *prayerful endurance*. We live in a fast paced society, and we are bombarded by sound bites and video clips. We have a very short attention span; it's often hard for us to focus on one thing for very long. Just as a swimmer needs to practice holding his breath underwater, so you must practice spending time in prayer.

So set a stopwatch, use an egg timer, or just look at a clock on the wall to make sure you get your fifteen minutes in. This "time barrier" will protect you from many distractions you might face. If you're eleven minutes into prayer and the phone rings, or you remember something you need to do, you can say to yourself that you'll get right to it … in four minutes.

I'd like you to do this for twenty-one days in a row. Why twenty-one? Because many psychologists tell us that any activity repeated for twenty-one days becomes a habit. I'd like to get you into the habit of prayer.

This is where humility comes in. You are *learning* to pray. I'm not saying you should pray fifteen minutes with three minutes per prayer form for the rest of your life. I'm saying you should do it for the next twenty-one days so that it comes to you naturally. These are the fundamentals of prayer. And this kind of pattern is good to go back to in those times in your life when you get spiritually out of sync, or you don't feel like praying.

Some days it will be easy. Others will be hard. But don't short-change the experience, even on the days when you don't feel like doing it. Those are the most important days to stay strong! Don't worry, we all have times like that. It's a test for us to see if we will be faithful even if we don't feel like it. Growing strong in Christ is not just about experiencing warm fuzzies and nice emotions. It can be hard to follow him but never impossible, thanks to his grace.

The football player who works out only when he feels like it will never make it to the National Football League. The dancer who dances only when she feels like it will never dance with the New York City Ballet. The guitarist who plays only when he has nothing else to do will never become a professional. And Christians who pray only when they feel like it will never become saints. Nor will they ever know the depth of God's love for them, or the amazing life to which they are called.

This race we run is not a sprint, but a marathon. It's a little bit each day. If we are to be *disciples,* then we must have *discipline.* This is how we train ourselves for religion. This is how we become spiritually strong. This is how we work out.

Be humble.
Be disciplined.
Begin.

What Should I Do Now?

HERE WE GO!!! For the next twenty-one days, spend your time in prayer like this:

CARDIOVASCULAR—Blessing and Adoration (three minutes)
- We receive God's blessings
- We respond by blessing God
- We come before him in adoration

FAT-BURNING—Petition (three minutes)
- We ask forgiveness
- We pray for his kingdom and his will
- We pray for our needs

MUSCLE-TONING—Intercession (three minutes)
- We "lift up" others
- We pray specifically and generally

STRETCH—Thanksgiving (three minutes)
- We open our eyes to what he has done for us
- We thank him, even for struggles that bring us closer to him

BREATHE—Praise (three minutes)
- We praise his name and love him for who he is

Remember, three minutes is a guideline, and if you feel like spending more time, then go for it! You are communicating with God, so make sure you let *him* communicate with *you*. If you feel his presence, just stop what you are doing and be with him.

FIVE

Staying Healthy

Being physically healthy and strong is all about diet and exercise. But disease and wounds can get in the way of this. By this point, we've covered how you can spiritually nourish yourself as well as how to spiritually work out. You should be praying regularly now; don't think you need to finish this book to begin. So if you're reading this but haven't done your fifteen minutes yet, or haven't been nourished by God in some way, then stop reading and start praying.

We'll be here when you get done.

I t's the punch line at the end of a long lament. A person goes on and on about all the horrible things in his or her life, but finishes with, "at least I've got my health." It's a statement that no matter what happens outside our body, we can handle it if we are healthy inside.

Sickness can weaken and even kill us, no matter how strong our muscles are or how well our heart is beating. Light sicknesses can slow us down; serious ones can leave us bedridden or dead. As a country, we spend billions of dollars on researching disease. We've cured many ailments, but many more remain a threat. Much of the time, we struggle with ignorance. We don't know if there is a virus in the air, so we can't avoid catching it. We don't know how to cure many diseases, so we just treat the symptoms.

Gaining knowledge is a big help toward growing in health.

Though we don't know enough to let everyone live in perfect health every day of their lives, we do know a bit about staying healthy and avoiding disease. And this is why we spend so much time and money on research. We don't just want to know how to cure cancer, we also want to know what causes cancer so we can avoid getting it.

But knowledge is not enough. Take smoking, for example. We know that cigarettes kill people. More people die from cigarettes than from AIDS, murder, suicide, fires, alcohol, and all illegal drugs *combined*. And smokers are admitted to the hospital twice as often as nonsmokers (you can get these and even more facts at www.thetruth.com). Heck, there's even a huge warning on every box. Yet it's estimated that about 3,000 people (most under the age of eighteen) start smoking every day. And millions of others, who have heard it's dangerous, continue to smoke without even trying to stop. Clearly, *knowledge* is not enough. It is the first step, but must be followed by putting that knowledge into *practice*.

It's the same with our soul, but the stakes are even higher. Physical sickness leads to physical death. But spiritual sickness leads to spiritual death. While our physical sickness may make us die sooner than if we were healthy, the reality is that we will *all* physically die. It's just a matter of when. But not so with our souls. With Jesus Christ, *we will never have to die*. We can live with him forever.

Spiritual sickness, unlike much physical sickness, is not a mystery: God has given us knowledge of what to avoid as well as a cure for every ailment. You can't mysteriously catch a spiritual virus like you would catch a cold. But just as in physical sickness, the key to spiritual health is knowledge and practice. Specifically, for a healthy spiritual life we need to understand what sin is and how we can combat it. So let's talk about the nature of sin, what it does, what God did to get rid of it, and how we can avoid it from now on.

The Nature of Sin

What sickness is to our bodies, sin is to our souls. Sickness rebels against the health of our bodies, which is our life. Sin rebels against the God who loves us, who is the source of our life. Let's look at where sin began to find out more about what it is. It doesn't take long for Scripture to deal with the subject. On page one of the Bible we see God creating humanity. By about page two, humanity is starting to sin.

As God created the world, he repeated the phrase, "It is good." After he created humanity, he looked at "all he had made and indeed "it was *very* good" (Gn 1:31, emphasis mine). There was (and is) nothing wrong in what God created. There was no sin. This is seen in the nakedness of the first man and woman, Adam and Eve (which are Hebrew words literally meaning "man" and "woman"). "Now, both of them were naked, the man and his wife, but they felt no shame before each other" (Gn 2:25).

Enter the serpent. The serpent tempts Adam and Eve to break the only commandment that God gave: "But of the tree of the knowledge of good and evil you are not to eat; for, the day you eat of that, you are doomed to die" (Gn 2:17). We'll talk about the devil later, but the important thing right now is that you see that the serpent *did not force them to break God's law*. God said if they ate of that fruit, they would die. The serpent said that God lied, and told them that if they ate the fruit, "You will be like gods, knowing good from evil" (Gn 3:5). They believed the snake, and desired "the wisdom" the fruit would give. Eve ate it and handed it to Adam, who also ate. They made a choice. It began by not trusting God. It ended by leaving paradise.

What was so bad about eating a piece of fruit? Why would it lead to this terrible conclusion? The answer lies in the nature of the fruit and the nature of the fruit helps us understand the nature of sin. The fruit was called "the knowledge of good and evil." You might think this wouldn't be such a bad thing to know, but it's crucial to understand that it wasn't just the ability to know what is right and what is wrong. Adam and Eve already knew that since they were created in the image and likeness of God.

What the fruit offered was *the ability to decide for themselves* what is good and what is evil. Meaning that if God said something is evil,

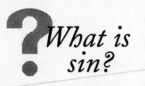 *What is sin?*

they could now decide for themselves that it is actually good. This is sin: God tells us to go one way, we decide to go another. This leads to death because God is Truth and we are not. God says, "Don't walk off that cliff or you'll die," and we say, "I don't think so." We don't trust him. We want to be like gods but we're not.

St. Paul talks about people "whose consciences are branded as though with a red-hot iron" (1 Tm 4:2). Simply put, sin hardens the soul. The more we do it, the more it numbs us. Being made in the image of God, who is good, we have a hard time doing things we know to be evil. Our bodies shake, our guilt kicks in, and our soul cries, "STOP!" So we convince ourselves that what is evil in God's sight is actually good. Then we can go through with it. And the more we do it, the easier it gets.

An extreme example of this is Adolph Hitler who was responsible for the slaughter of millions and millions of people. How could he mastermind such a horrendous plan? Because he convinced himself that what he was doing was good. The Jews deserved to die, he reasoned. So did Catholics, homosexuals, and anyone else who would taint "the master race."

Do you see the deceptive power of this disease? It makes us think our wrong actions are right actions. This wouldn't make a difference if life were a matter of opinion, but it's not. There is such a thing as truth. There is such a thing as reality. Jump off a bridge and I don't care how much you think you'll fly, the law of gravity will win.

Now some of you might be thinking, "Well, some people might die. But what if I had a hang glider or a parachute? Then I'd be safe." EVERYBODY THINKS THAT. Everybody thinks they're exempt from the rules. It's like the smoker who says, "I know that cigarettes kill people, but they won't kill me." They believe a lie because they want to smoke. We believe lies because we want to sin. The serpent told Adam and Eve that they wouldn't die, and they believed it because they wanted to be like gods. They listened and they brought death into the world.

We all think that someone else will get caught cheating, someone else will get a sexually transmitted disease, someone else will get alcohol poisoning. But even if we do escape the physical consequences of our actions, we can never hide from the spiritual results. The word sin literally means "without." Sin causes us to live without God. And if we die in this state, we die "without" him forever.

The Results of Sin

We will spend eternity in one of two places. We will either live forever with God in heaven, or live forever apart from God in hell. There are many who don't believe that hell exists, probably for the same reasons we think smoking won't kill us or we can be sexually active without contracting an STD: We think it doesn't exist because *we don't want it to exist*. But heaven and hell are not matters of opinion, and not believing in them doesn't make them go away.

? *If God is good, then why does hell exist?*

Hell exists as a result of humanity's decision to be its own god and not follow God. Some ask why, if God is so loving, he allows hell to exist. Ironically, it's because he is so loving that hell exists. Let me explain.

The great gift God gave to humanity is freedom. He never forced us to love him. That's why he provided an opportunity to turn against him (the Tree of the Knowledge of Good and Evil) and a place to go if we don't want to be with him (hell). To force his love upon us would not be love at all. He gives us a choice, and respects our choice. If there were no hell, there could be no real love. If everyone had to end up with him eternally, then we could never choose him.

Now, let me simplify heaven and hell for you, because our culture has so many false images and stereotypes. Heaven is often pictured as a vacation, like lying on a beach. Hell is pictured as an annoyance, like a refrigerator filled with cookies but no milk. Or even worse, heaven is seen as boring while hell is imagined to be a huge party. Neither view is true.

Heaven is being fully with God, and hell is being fully without him. God is love. He is light. He is fulfillment. He is peace. Heaven, then, is the ultimate experience of these things as we live in his presence and participate in his life. Hell is the opposite: hatred, darkness, emptiness, despair.

Heaven is a million times better than anything we could imagine, and hell is a million times worse. It's key to understand that heaven and hell depend not on a *place* but on a *person*. Heaven is being with God. People who want to follow God go (by his grace) to where he is forever. People who don't follow God go where he has allowed himself not to be. God respects their decision.

It's not like choosing where you want to visit over spring break. It's more like choosing the person you want to marry, the one you want to be with for the rest of your existence. People who think of heaven as a *place* think they'll sneak in because they heard somewhere that God loves them, and they figure that they're not as bad as a lot of other people on the earth. Yes, God loves everyone, but we must choose to love him back to have a relationship with him. Sin is humanity's way of saying to God, "We don't want you in our lives." The tragic consequence is that God responds by sadly saying, "OK."

And so we live "without."

God doesn't send people to hell. Our sins send us to hell. It is God who saves us from this place we're heading, but he can only save us if we follow him.

The Cure

When sin entered the world, it destroyed our chance to have an intimate relationship with God. It cut us off from the source of life. God had every right to walk away from us, but he didn't. When we were faithless, he was faithful. When we were sinful, he was merciful. When we gave him death, he gave us life.

At the center of all time and history is the death and resurrection of Jesus Christ. Everything that happened before led to that moment; everything that has happened since has pointed back to it. The world asked God how much he loves us, and Jesus stretched out his arms and he died.

Scripture tells us, "For the wage paid by sin is death; the gift freely given by God is eternal life in Christ Jesus our Lord" (Rom 6:23). Sin brought death into the world. God overcame the results of sin so that through him we might have life. He reached out to a humanity that was destined for hell, and opened the gates of heaven by his own blood.

As his dead body hung upon the cross, a soldier pierced his side and blood and water flowed from it. This blood and water was the beginning of the life of the church: baptism and Eucharist.

Understand his plan of salvation for us: the Father created the plan, the Son put it into effect, and the Holy Spirit makes it effective. It's like building a vacuum cleaner. The Father makes the blueprints, the Son puts it together, and the Holy Spirit is the electricity that makes it run.

What they built was the church. When you read Scripture, the church was not an afterthought, or a creation of people after Jesus left. God has empowered the church with the means to be salvation to the world, and the specific way it brings about God's life is through the sacraments.

The sacraments are acts of God that make him physically present in our reality. We have spoken of the Eucharist already: the bread and the wine become the Body and Blood of Jesus Christ. Though the Eucharist is considered the Sacrament of sacraments, the most necessary sacrament is baptism, because without it no other sacrament can be received.

In this sacrament, our new life begins in the name of the Trinity as we are cleansed with holy water. Water is a sign of life and of death. The Israelites were led by Moses through the Red Sea so that they could be safe, but the sea closed in on the Egyptians and killed them. So too, in the waters of our baptism we are led out of slavery into the safety of the family of God, with our sin destroyed behind us.

We are all born with traits from our parents. If one of your parents had a genetically-based disease, it was most likely passed on from an ancestor. Since Adam and Eve brought sin into the world, all humanity has suffered from it. In baptism, we find the cure to this deadly disease and enter into a relationship with God.

The fruits of that relationship are seen in the Eucharist, where we physically participate in his life. Confirmation matures the graces we received in baptism so that we can be strong in our faith. When we get sick, we have reconciliation (for our soul) and anointing of the sick (for our body). We only receive baptism once, but to be freed of other sins, we go to reconciliation to return to the waters of our baptism (something we also do every time we walk into church and bless ourselves with holy water). These sacraments equip us with God's grace to live a holy, single life for him. If God calls us to be with another or to the priesthood, he gives us grace through the sacraments of marriage or holy orders.

Participating in the sacraments is how we are "cured" from our separation with God, and how we can participate in his life to stay healthy. Some sacraments we can receive over and over (like the Eucharist, reconciliation, and anointing of the sick), while others we receive only once (baptism, confirmation, and holy orders). The church doesn't just want you to *receive* the sacraments, but to *live* them. You can't be rebaptized, but you can live the life of grace that baptism has opened up to you. You *can* receive the Eucharist, even every day. The more you receive him, the more you'll be like him.

We have the gift of God to be freed from sin, so how can we avoid sin? Even though baptism has washed us clean, we are still left with something the church calls *concupiscence*. That means though our body has been cleansed of the disease, it is weak from the damage caused by wrong living. We feel that weakness as we try to live holy lives, and struggle with our sin.

Yet we are not without hope, because "for God everything is possible" (Mk 10:27). He has won the victory that we have lost, and he is inviting us to share in it through his death and resurrection. The more attached we become to him, the more detached we are from sin. And since he has freed us from its grasp, we can learn ways to avoid it as well.

We must put what we *know* into how we *live*. Those two things, *knowledge* and *action*, are essential parts of staying healthy with God.

Step One: Believing God

There is a difference between *knowing* and *doing*, between *believing* and *following*. We begin with belief in what we know: "I could win the lottery." Based on that belief, we buy a ticket. We act out what we believe. If we didn't ever buy a ticket, people might question the level of our belief.

But lottery tickets only cost a dollar. It's not a big risk. What if lottery tickets cost ten dollars? Do we believe that much? What if they were one hundred dollars? What if they were one thousand dollars? Suddenly, the casual believer is thrown, because the risk of following through could have disastrous consequences.

I know many who say they believe in God. But when you get practical about following him, they bail. Spend time in prayer each day? Don't get drunk? Do charitable works? No sex before marriage? I don't believe *that* much, they might say. It's easy to believe in something when the stakes are low. But God wants our life. To give it to him, we need to really trust him with it.

Sin begins with a lack of trust in God. We turn to sin because of things we need (or think we need) in life: we need to be loved, we need to be accepted, we need to be healed of our pain, and so on. Yet many believe the lie that God does not want what is best for them, or is even out to get them.

But this is not what we see in Jesus Christ. He said, "The thief comes only to steal and kill and destroy. I have come so that they may have life and have it to the full" (Jn 10:10). What an incredible statement! The very things that some people think give them life are the things that kill them. Jesus has come to offer us a better life, a life to the full. The idea that followers of Christ don't "live it up" as much as others do is a lie. As Christians, we can live life 100 percent because we follow the One who created it.

Just because we are in possession of this life doesn't mean we're the ones who best know how to live it. I own a computer, but I must confess that I don't really know how it works. My finger hits a key, the letter appears on the screen, and I don't question how it happens. I can do some basic stuff, but when things start crashing I'm on the phone to people who know how this thing was *made*. It's *my* computer, but if I want to use it to its fullest potential I need to talk to the folks who built it. It's the same with our lives.

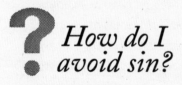

How do I avoid sin?

Adam and Eve didn't trust God when he told them they would die. But their actions said so much more than that. They not only didn't trust his curse, they also implied that they didn't trust his blessings either. It was as though they didn't believe that he was letting them live the best life possible. They thought that maybe this God was holding something back from them, and maybe they thought they could do a better job on their own.

The first step in avoiding sin in your life is to trust God. You must *believe* that he wants to bless you. You must know that you have a purpose in life that only he can fulfill. If you are not certain of the One who leads you, then you'll start to question how he leads you, and you'll never get anywhere.

Meditate, and even memorize, these words from God to help your heart trust him more: "Yes, I know what plans I have in mind for you, Yahweh declares, plans for peace, not for disaster, to give you a future and a hope" (Jer 29:11). And Jesus tells us that, "I have come so that they may have life and have it to the full" (Jn 10:10). Whatever he asks us to do and whatever he asks us to avoid have one purpose: to *bless* us. Knowing that is the first step.

Step Two: Following Through
If believing that God wants what is best for us is the first step in overcoming sin, then following him is the next step. And it's a tough one because it's only when we try to get rid of sin that we realize the kind of power it has over us. Check out the words of St. Paul and see if you don't relate:

> *I do not understand my own behaviour: I do not act as I mean to, but I do things that I hate.... The good thing I want to do, I never do; the evil thing which I do not want—that is what I do.... So I find this rule: that for me, where I want to do nothing but good, evil is close at my side. In my inmost self I dearly love God's law, but I see that acting on my body there is a different law which battles against the law in my mind.... What a wretched man I am! Who will rescue me from this body doomed to death? God—thanks be to him—through Jesus Christ our Lord.*
>
> ROMANS 7:15, 19, 21-25

Our very lives become a *struggle* with sin. It is not unusual that you would have these struggles, in fact it is what faith is about. Don't be surprised that there is sin in your life. Don't be surprised that it keeps coming back, even when you kick it out again and again. Don't think that because you struggle with sin it means you can't be holy.

Let me illustrate what holiness is (and isn't) by using the example of *colors*. There are two different rules for colors: one for pigment (paint or physical stuff) and one for light. For pigment, the primary colors are red, yellow, and blue. If you want to make black, you blend all those colors together equally. If you want white, you need to remove all those colors completely. This is often how people see holiness. Holiness is white. In pigment, white is the absence of other things. So holiness is seen as the absence of sin. And any additional color makes it not white. It is almost impossible to get pure white ... just like it seems impossible to be holy.

But God is from the heavens, not from the earth. And though the ground gives us pigment, the sky gives us light. The color rules for light are different. First, the primary colors are yellow, cyan, and magenta. So we're already using different colors than that of earth. But the most important difference is in how we achieve black and white. To get black, you remove all color and get darkness. To get white, you add all the colors together and make the brightest light possible.

Holiness is like white light. Whereas pigment naturally tends toward black, light tend toward white. Whereas white pigment is based on what you *don't* have, white light is based on what you *do* have. Whereas some people think that holiness is just the absence of sin, it's really about the presence of grace. And when you've got that in your life, you shine.

Light overcomes darkness as holiness overcomes sin. It is sin that is that darkness, the "without." Darkness cannot overpower light, but light can dispel the dark. Light a small candle in a dark room to see what I mean.

Do we wish to live in perfect light? Yes, that is what we look forward to in heaven. But the shadow of our sin cannot extinguish the candle of faith, unless we blow it out ourselves. We do that by not asking for forgiveness (or not allowing ourselves to be forgiven). That you will fall many times in your walk with Christ is not a question. The question is this: will you let him pick you up? HE WILL DO IT EVERY TIME, if you let him.

On the night he was killed, Jesus was betrayed both by Judas and by Peter. One did not repent and hanged himself. The other said he was sorry, and continued to follow. One became one of history's most famous sinners, the other became the rock of our church and one of her greatest saints. The difference hinged not on what they did, but on how they came to God—or failed to come to God—after they did it.

It's the same with you. It is imperative that you get rid of sinful behaviors in your life, but your relationship with Jesus is not based on that. As Pope John Paul II once said, "We are not the sum of our weaknesses and failures; we are the sum of the Father's love for us and our real capacity to become the image of his Son."

To follow God means that every time you fall down, you get back up. And it means that you *act:* you pray, you do works of charity, you gather with other Christians, you go to church and so forth. Living our faith is more than just not sinning.

At the heart of it all is prayer. That's why your spiritual workout is so important. The more you seek the face of Christ, the less you will seek the sin. We surrender all our actions, the good and the bad, to Jesus Christ on the cross, and pray that he will transform them into something greater than we could ever imagine.

Sin is about lacking something, so you should "do" something to be freed from it. To sit around trying to "not do" something almost encourages you to do it, because you're thinking about it all the time. What can you do instead? Don't just say "no" to sin, say "yes" to God. He will heal your wounds and strengthen your muscles. He will keep you healthy if you stay focused on him.

Two Great Tips for Overcoming Sin

1. Trust that God is stronger. Here's a really good verse to commit to memory: "None of the trials which have come upon you is more than a human being can stand. You can trust that God will not let you be put to the test beyond your strength, but with any trial will also provide a way out by enabling you to put up with it" (1 Cor 10:13). You cannot be overpowered by sin. He will show you a way out, if you're looking for it.

2. Eat something. Yes, you heard me right. We sin because we are *hungry*. I'm not talking about physical hunger, but spiritual hunger. When we don't nourish ourselves enough with God, we start seeking satisfaction in other areas. I know some who try to pray through such episodes, usually with little success. It would be like a person doing push-ups to fill an empty stomach. When tempted, don't just say "no" to the sin, but replace it with a "yes" for God! Read some Scripture, listen to some worship music, get in your car and drive to church to pray before the Eucharist, or call a friend and experience some fellowship.

What Should I Do Now?

You should give yourself a "Spiritual Checkup," or an examination of conscience. It's found at the end of this book. The sacrament of reconciliation is the best way to stay in a healthy relationship with God, and our bishops suggest we receive it once a month. There's a section at the end of the book on how to go ("The Ultimate Fat-Burning Exercise"). Most churches offer reconciliation on Saturday afternoon, and sometimes you can find one that offers it daily. Make it a monthly habit to get right with God. If you haven't been recently, then make plans to go!

SIX

The Battle of Prayer

If prayer is so simple, then why do so few do it? Well, something that is simple is not necessarily easy. For example, I could tell you to hold your arms up and keep them there. Simple? Yes. Easy? Well, for a few seconds it is. A minute later it gets a lot harder. Ten minutes later it is extremely difficult. An hour? Forget about it.

Though prayer may be simple in nature, it can be difficult in practice. The Catechism explains it beautifully: "Prayer is both a gift of grace and a determined response on our part. It always presupposes effort" (CCC 2725). Simply put, prayer is hard and we need to work at it. The Catechism goes on to say what we have learned from people who have dedicated their lives to this effort: "Prayer is a battle."

Too many people don't realize that prayer takes work. They want prayer to be a comfortable time where they get to feel good about themselves. They want the results of prayer (holiness) without actually praying.

This is a reflection of our American society. The most effective way to be healthy and lose weight is to eat healthy foods and exercise regularly. But we don't want to do that. We want to eat what we want and not spend time exercising, but still lose weight and look good. So we look for the "Miracle Weight Loss Pill," or the diets that boast, "Eat whatever you want and still lose weight!" We wear clothing that tightens our flab, or we walk around sucking in our gut. We would rather go through surgery than sacrifice. I've even seen ads for the "Abdomizer," a belt that you put around your abs that fires electronic shocks into them, causing them to flex and simulate a workout. And you can do it while eating potato chips and watching TV!

Bluntly put, we cheat. We want the result without the effort. We want the destination without the journey. We don't ask, "What can I do to please God?" but instead, "How much can I get away with before God gets mad at me?" (especially regarding sexual sins). In short, our culture encourages doing as little as possible to get as much as possible, even if we don't deserve it.

If we embrace this cultural mentality, we find it almost impossible to lead a spiritual life because there are no shortcuts with our soul. There is no cheating. We're dealing with a God who knows *everything*. You can't fake being holy. You might be able to get away with it in front of others, but you never for a moment fool God. When we come before God, we can't look at the answers we wrote in the palm of our hand, offer a note from our doctor, or look for a loophole to explain why we're an exception to the rule. At the end of our lives he will ask, "Did you love me?"

The fruit of our love for Jesus is expressed in our prayer life. It makes sense, really. Can you say you love him and not spend time with him? We make time for friendships, school activities, TV shows, and Internet chat rooms. But if we don't put God first in our life and give him our time, it shows that we don't love him as much as we say we do.

Prayer is difficult because it makes us take a hard look at who we are and what we do. We look in the mirror and don't always like what we see. Our first reaction is to put on a mask to cover the ugliness we perceive to be there. But the face behind that mask is the one that God loves. And when we try to be something we're not, we close ourselves off to him. He loves you as you are. And his love will change you, if you are willing to love him back.

In the physical body, there are two main deterrents to growing strong: wounds and weaknesses. A person with a broken arm can't do push-ups. And a person with weak legs can't run miles on end (at least not at first). In our soul, we also fight wounds and weaknesses. Our wounds are the sins we do that hurt ourselves and our relationship with God. Our weaknesses are patterns in our life that are not necessarily sinful, but can still distract us from our goal (and also lead us into sin).

As we fight this battle, we must address both. The good news in Christ is this: our wounds can be healed and our weaknesses strengthened. They will cause you to fall, but the key to the Christian life is to allow Christ to raise you up every time that you fall down. If a runner runs an almost perfect race but falls at the end and doesn't get up, he will be defeated by the runner who fell twenty times but got up after each one.

Did you know that when you break a bone in the body (and allow it to properly heal), the place where it heals becomes stronger than the rest of the bone? God does this in our soul, too. Jesus can transform something that takes us away from him into something that draws us closer. This is why St. Paul said, "It is, then, about my weaknesses that I am happiest of all to boast, so that the power of Christ may rest upon me.... For it is when I am weak that I am strong" (2 Cor 12:9-10).

There are four things we all fight in this battle of prayer: the devil, distraction, dryness, and despair. These can weaken and even wound us, but when we surrender them to Christ's power they can turn us into saints.

The Devil

Yes, there is such a thing as the devil. He's not some fairy tale. He is very real. The devil is known as "the lord of lies," so let me share some truths that will help you in your battle with him.

First of all, the devil is not as powerful as God. God is all-knowing, all-powerful, and everywhere. The devil does not know everything, does not have all the power, and is not everywhere. The devil cannot get into your brain and read your thoughts, unless you are foolish enough to open your mind to him. The devil cannot make you do things, unless you invite him into your life.

The devil? Isn't that a myth?

And the devil is not everywhere, so that you can find no place to rest.

Though the devil is not all-knowing, he is very, very smart. Much smarter than you or me. Though the devil is not all-powerful, he is much stronger than any human. And though he isn't everywhere, he certainly covers more territory than we do.

Were it not for God, we wouldn't stand a chance. You should be aware, but not terrified, of the devil. Think of him as a raging animal in a cage. Were it not for the cage, you'd be his food. Unfortunately, we have the power to open that cage, and we too often do—with devastating results.

Where did the devil come from? God created him. He was an angel who rebelled against God. Why did God allow him to rebel? The same reason he allows us to, because he offers us free will to choose him or reject him. So then, why does God let the devil exist?

A better question is this: *Why do we?*

God protects us by making the devil play by the same rules he does. He can only come in if we let him. We can be tempted, but not forced to sin. Remember God's promise: "God will not let you be put to the test beyond your strength, but with any trial will also provide a way out by enabling you to put up with it" (1 Cor 10:13).

The way to beat the devil is not by your own strength, but by surrendering to God. The devil will do everything in his power to keep you from prayer, but he isn't strong enough when you ask for God's help and are willing to make sacrifices to receive it.

Don't be afraid. Jesus spoke and demons fled. The devil tries to destroy us because he is not powerful enough to destroy God. But God has already won the victory through the resurrection of Christ! The day the devil thought was his ultimate victory became his eternal defeat. And now we as followers of Christ share in that resurrection, and by doing so are freed from the devil's grasp.

Scripture tells us, "Never, when you are being put to the test, say, 'God is tempting me'; God cannot be tempted by evil, and he does not put anybody to the test. Everyone is put to the test by being attracted and seduced by that person's own wrong desire" (Jas 1:13-14). We only respond to the sinful desires of our heart. The devil might offer the sin, but we are the ones who find it attractive.

So as Christians we can never say, "The devil made me do it." Though we are freed from Satan's grasp, we still fight him every day. St. Peter tells us that the devil "is on the prowl like a roaring lion, looking for someone to devour" (1 Pt 5:8). So should we run away? No, says Peter: "Stand up to him, solid in faith.... You will have to suffer for only a little while: the God of all grace who called you to eternal glory in Christ will restore you, he will confirm, strengthen and support you" (1 Pt 5:9-10). When we rely on the power of God, we partake in the victory of Christ.

It would be easy for us to blame the devil for what we do wrong, and take the credit for all we do that is good. Yet we are responsible for our own decisions, and that is what gives us the ability to truly love God. Even when we "let the devil out of the cage," God is still stronger when we repent and submit our lives to him. He can handle the devil.

Distraction

So I'm kneeling in prayer and saying the Our Father, and I think about my own father. He's going to take me to a football game next month. Next month is October. That means Halloween is coming up. My favorite costume when I was little was Spiderman. "Spiderman, Spiderman, does whatever a spider can."

In about five seconds I can go from praying the words Jesus taught me to singing a cartoon theme. So I get mad at myself for being so spacey and I tell myself to stop thinking of that song. Or the cartoon. Or the movie, which I thought was pretty good. But not as good as *Star Wars*. The best was when Yoda fought with his lightsaber. I'd have a green lightsaber if I were a Jedi. I wish I were a Jedi. Natalie Portman is cute. Was I just praying something?

It happens to all of us. Our imagination can run amuck. The Catechism confirms something we all know: "The habitual difficulty in prayer is *distraction*" (CCC 2729). We begin in faith but end in fantasy. Now don't focus on your distractions, because that will only make it worse. But when you find yourself distracted, take a moment to learn from these random thoughts. They often have something to offer you.

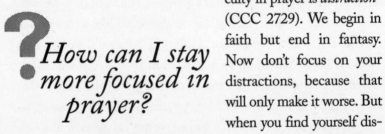

How can I stay more focused in prayer?

If you find your imagination is destroying your prayer life, then I suggest that you aren't using it correctly. It can be like stubborn children on a baseball team; if they're not allowed to play on the field, then they will yell, scream, and knock things over in the dugout until they get their turn at bat. The same is true in prayer. If you don't *use* your imagination in prayer, it will turn against you.

Our imagination is a gift from God that helps us encounter the things our senses don't experience, or relive those we do. With it, we can hear and sing in a symphony of praise, we can see the smile on the face of God, and we touch the hem of his garment. Scripture can come alive as we put ourselves in the middle of the story. By the use of our imagination, we can be dancing with the angels or praying at the foot of the cross.

But what we imagine and what we allow to distract us often reveal what our heart is attached to. Distractions reveal our inmost desires, and teach us about the battle our heart is going through to surrender itself to God. What is it that we are putting before him? Is it material things? Is it fame or popularity? Is it a relationship we're in (or wish we were in)?

What distracts us in prayer can often be a sign of what distracts us in life. And how we pray will affect how we live. If we can, in prayer, offer those desires to God and make him first and foremost, then the same will occur in our daily lives.

Of course, one last reason we get distracted is because we are lazy and we approach prayer, and even God, far too casually. When God tells us he wants a relationship with us and he wants to be our friend, we often reduce him to our level. Yes, he is our friend, but he is still GOD. The Bible tells us that "fear of [the Lord] is the beginning of knowledge" (Prv 1:7). *Fear of the Lord* refers to the awe and respect that God deserves (it's not like terror or horror). It makes us realize that *he* came for *us* and *we* live for *him*. It is not the other way around.

The word the church uses for this kind of lax attitude in prayer is *acedia* or spiritual sloth. What is needed is a renewed determination and vigilance when we approach God. A helpful hint: just as we must focus our mind in prayer, we must also focus our body. Our body position is very important. It can greatly help, or greatly hinder, our efforts. Standing, kneeling, praying with our hands raised, or just sitting in an attentive way can often snap out us of our laziness. We should be conscious of what our body is doing, and let it participate in our prayer. Never forget that mind, body, and soul are all connected.

Distractions offer us a choice. "Therein lies the battle; the choice of which master to serve" (CCC 2729). They are not just an ingredient for failure, but an opportunity for holiness. By understanding what distracts us in prayer, we can understand what separates us from God, and by surrendering that to him we can draw closer (and more *attracted*) than ever before.

Dryness

In 1979, Fr. Thomas Green wrote a book about prayer called *When the Well Runs Dry*. It's about how to handle periods of time when we don't "feel anything" in prayer. The title says it all. He didn't call the book *If the Well Runs Dry* but *When*. Everybody goes through it.

? Why don't I feel like praying sometimes?

In fact, *we have to* experience this kind of dryness if we are ever to truly grow in our relationship with God. Many times, our deeper conversion to Jesus is filled with (and often fueled by) emotion. We realize the immense love of God, and the freedom from sin that he offers. We pray and we feel so good, it's like he wraps his arms around us. In short, we get a kind of spiritual high.

A few days or weeks later, that high goes away. This doesn't mean that you've done something wrong—it can actually mean the opposite: dryness in prayer is a sign that you are drawing closer to him! We shouldn't treat God as a spiritual drug pusher, expecting to get high every time we come to him. If that were the case, everybody would pray all the time, but would do so for all the wrong reasons. In periods of dryness, you have a chance to show that your commitment to him is real. And it is in those moments that our prayer can be the most powerful, because we do it based on choice rather than on emotion. It is a chance to love God for who he is rather than for what he does for us.

The best thing to do when you face this struggle is to keep praying. Go to the fundamentals of prayer (the five forms of the spiritual workout). Think of it as if you are following a runner through the night who is carrying a torch. If that runner goes over a hill, it might seem like he disappeared. To stop and wonder where he went will only slow your discovery of where he is. If you keep running on the path you were on, you'll get to the top of the hill and find him again.

There is a chance, however, that you don't see him because you are off course. Sometimes we feel separated from God because we *are* separated from God. If there is unrepented sin in your life, it can make it difficult to experience his love. I know of those who tried to follow God but also thought they could keep destroying their body with drugs, stay in sexual relationships, or embrace other things contrary to his will. They didn't make it long. A rope can only be pulled so far before it snaps you back. Saying yes to God can be easy. Saying no to the things that are not of God is the real challenge.

The key word here is *unrepented* sin. This refers to sin that you don't say you are sorry for, sin that you don't think is wrong to do, and sin that you have no intention of giving up. I'm not talking about the sin we *struggle* with; I'm talking about the sin we *surrender* to. You will fight with sin until the day you die, but that sin will never separate you from the love of God. The love that Jesus showed us on the cross will never be diminished by any bad thing you can do. But if you don't ask for his mercy, you will shut yourself off from his presence.

Dryness in prayer offers us an opportunity to show our commitment to God. We can do this by choosing prayer over our emotions (we pray though we don't feel anything) or by choosing God over our sinfulness. The choice is ours, the grace is his. If we persevere in prayer, we will feel him again. But we will also realize that our emotions aren't the most important thing in our relationship with God.

Despair

Here's a tough one, perhaps the most difficult one of all. We pray and pray for something and it hasn't happened yet, or something occurs that makes it clear that it will never happen at all. We start to wonder if God is listening, or if he cares, or if he even has the power to do what we ask of him. We fall into despair.

> **?** *Why hasn't God answered a prayer of mine?*

Despair is when we look at the entire prayer process and wonder, "What's the point?" It is often brought on by unanswered (or denied) intentions or petitions that we have brought before God.

The Catechism, while dealing with this question, poses an interesting thought: "When we praise God or give him thanks for his benefits in general, we are not particularly concerned whether or not our prayer is acceptable to him. On the other hand, we demand to see the results of our petitions. What is the image of God that motivates our prayer: an instrument to be used, or the Father of our Lord Jesus Christ?" (CCC 2735).

Scripture makes it clear that often we don't see results because, "[We] prayed wrongly, wanting to indulge [our] passions" (Jas 4:3). Prayer is not based on *getting*, but on *giving*. I know of some who have gone so far as to make their prayer a threat: "If I don't get a boyfriend, I'll never pray again." That might sound silly, but we can all be guilty of such prayers.

Like distraction, despair can help us to understand the depths of our heart. How must God prove himself to me if I am to keep praying? Is what I am asking of God a righteous and reasonable thing, or am I just trying to use him? What is it I am *really* asking for, and is he giving it to me in ways I don't expect?

That last question is key. For example, many who pray for a dating relationship are actually praying to be loved. Is God providing that love in other ways? Many who pray for success are really praying for self-worth. Can God be teaching me that I am more than what I do? We can be like hungry beggars who ask for filet mignon with mushroom sauce, and scoff when we get chicken or bread instead. We must trust him to satisfy our needs, and not be too particular about the way he chooses to do it. He is God, after all, and he does know *everything*. Could it be that his way may be better than ours?

Some of you have prayed for very serious things. You've prayed that your parents wouldn't get divorced, that abuse would stop, or that a loved one wouldn't die. To respond by giving clichés or cutesy sayings about prayer would only cheapen the emotional impact these events have had in your life, and I'm not about to do that.

But I can say this: *God does answer prayers.* And he does it in ways we often never expect. The life of Christ is a perfect example. God promised the Jews that someone would come to save them from their oppression. They figured that, since they were held captive by the Romans, God would send a great warrior king to kill the enemy and restore the nation to its former greatness. Instead, he came as a poor carpenter's son who was tortured and killed on a cross. Jesus did not free the Israelites from Rome, he freed humanity from the oppression of sin. He answered their prayer in a more powerful way, a way they never expected.

It may draw you closer to Jesus to know that he also struggled with unanswered prayer. As he knelt in the garden before they took him to be crucified, he prayed, "Father ... if you are willing, take this cup away from me." But then he added, "Nevertheless, let your will be done, not mine" (Lk 22:42). Jesus did not have a death wish. He was fully God, but also fully human. He did not want to die. He just wanted the Father's will more.

Though people will endure great suffering for something worthy, nobody *wants* it. A pregnant woman does not look forward to the pains of labor. Jesus did not *want* the nails driven into his wrists and feet, but he endured our sinfulness that we might be saved. In many ways, the world scars us as it did Jesus. He carries the nail marks, we carry the scars left by actions done by others or ourselves. As we look at those wounds and wonder why, or as we encounter those difficulties and pray not to face them, we must realize that we have a God who did the same.

But we must also see that God can take the bleakest situation and turn it into the best. God answers prayers in ways we don't expect, even sometimes after the fact. I cannot answer for all the sufferings of the world. I can only say we have a God who suffered, too. And it is this God who frees us from this life to be with him in the next, a place where it says that "He will wipe away all tears from their eyes; there will be no more death, and no more mourning or sadness or pain" (Rv 21:4).

We are asked to pray for God's will to be done because so often it is not. Though what you experienced might not have been the will of God, he can still take it and make something holy out of it, if you let him. This life is an unfair place where many innocent people have suffered, but none more innocent than Jesus Christ, the One who now calls us to follow him and be with him in prayer. The thing that was once used to execute criminals is now the central symbol of our faith. He transformed the cross, and he can transform you. He raised the dead days after they died. He freed us from sin thousands of years after we were condemned by it.

Do not give up hope in a God who can do things like that. No matter how dark it is, don't despair. He can heal you. He can redeem you. It can be shocking to realize that we have a God who is more interested in *redeeming* suffering than *relieving* suffering. He would rather use suffering to bring about holiness than just take suffering away. It would be cruel if he were unwilling to endure pain himself, but he showed us, two thousand years ago, how willing he was to suffer with us and for us. He does not leave us in those times, but instead draws us closer to his heart. When there is nothing else to cling to, we can cling most tightly to him.

This is the incredible love of God: in those moments we could be facing sorrow and pain alone, we find life with him instead. And often in ways we never expect.

Fight! Fight! Fight!

Prayer makes a difference. This knowledge is the most important weapon you can have in your battle of prayer. It is not positive thinking, or spiritual fantasy. It is becoming united with God in an intimate way.

Prayer is not optional. It *is* your life with Christ. Runners *run,* swimmers *swim,* dancers *dance,* and Christians *pray.* It's what you do. It's not about living a moral code, or being a nice person. It's about being in a relationship with God. This relationship is built on prayer.

Prayer works. Your life will change. You will be transformed. If you stay focused on Jesus, the devil will be defeated. Your distraction will turn into determination. Your dryness will deepen your desire. And moments of despair will become occasions of grace.

So do not give up! When you are tired, know that you pray with the strength of the Holy Spirit. Even in the midst of great suffering, you are never alone. Remember the faithful love of the One who calls you into his life. Yes, prayer is a battle, but he fights it with us! You can overcome all these things with Christ, the Good Shepherd of whom was written:

> *In grassy meadows he lets me lie.*
> *By tranquil streams he leads me to restore my spirit....*
> *Even were I to walk in a ravine as dark as death*
> *I should fear no danger, for you are at my side....*
> *You anoint my head with oil; my cup brims over.*
> *Kindness and faithful love pursue me every day of my life.*
>
> PSALM 23:2-6

St. Paul, reflecting on this awesome love of God, writes to encourage us in our fight of faith:

Do you not realize that, though all the runners in the stadium take part in the race, only one of them gets the prize? Run like that—to win. Every athlete concentrates completely on training, and this is to win a wreath that will wither, whereas ours will never wither. So that is how I run, not without a clear goal; and how I box, not wasting blows on air. I punish my body and bring it under control, to avoid any risk that, having acted as herald for others, I myself may be disqualified.

1 CORINTHIANS 9:24-27

Make no mistake: prayer is a battle. But it's one you can fight and it's one Christ will win. It's how we say "yes" to God. It's what we need to do to be like him.

What Should I Do Now?

Go and pray! Remember that you pray not by your own strength, but by the Holy Spirit. Ask God to help you in prayer, and focus on him as best you can. Keep your commitment to that sacred time, and give it your all.

SEVEN

Teammates

We just read about Paul comparing our faith life to that of running a race. Running is quite a simple process. You go from one foot to the other in rapid fashion. If you only ran on one foot, you'd make some progress, but you'd never move as fast as you could with both feet.

In prayer, we need to run with both feet as well. One foot is individual prayer. The other is prayer with a community. Yes, there are those rare souls called to live as hermits with no contact with the world around them, but even they will tell you of the importance of community.

It is by a community that we were created. Even from a biological standpoint, no human has ever been self-created, or created by one person alone (even test-tube babies needed a man's and a woman's donation to make their life possible). This simple fact of our natural life tells us something about our spiritual life.

None of us came to know Christ by ourselves. We were evangelized by community. Even if our only encounter with Christ was through Scripture, the early church *community* brought Scripture together. And though we eventually experience individual intimacy with our Savior, many people such as parents, youth ministers, priests, friends, and relatives help bring us to that point with the Lord.

And it is to a community we will go when we are done with this earthly life. The biblical vision of heaven depicts great numbers of people singing praise to God. Since heaven is a community, wouldn't it make sense that the best way to experience heaven on earth is by praying as a community?

It would, with one exception. Heaven is a perfect community. Earth is imperfect. But it is to this communal life that we are called, no matter how sinful or imperfect the community is. Much of the focus of this book has been on individual prayer, but the same principles apply to community prayer. You will find that communal worship will enhance your individual prayer time, and individual devotion will enhance your group prayer. As one foot propels the other, so do individual and communal prayer, until you find yourself running faster and faster into the arms of Jesus.

The Community of God

But why do we need other people? Why isn't "me and Jesus" good enough? I often hear people scoff at organized religion, as if being with other people distracts from true prayer to God. But there are

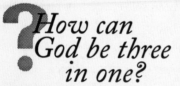
How can God be three in one?

two reasons why it is important that we pray with others. One, God *commands* us to be in community with each other. Two, God *is* community. Yes, you read that correctly. We believe in one God—the Father, Son, and Holy Spirit. The most Holy Trinity is, at heart, a community of love. God is love, but for love to be real, it can't just rest in itself. It must *give*. God shows us an example of this kind of life in the sacrament of marriage. I love my wife so intensely, and she returns that love, so much so that nine months later we give that love a name.

So God is three people? Not in the way we would normally use that word. The word "person" refers to the essence of someone, while the word "nature" refers to how they live that out. Every human being has a "person" and a "nature." Let me use my own humanity as an example.

I am a human *person* with a human *nature*. My human nature means that I don't flap my arms and fly, because that would be bird nature. It means I don't breathe underwater, because that would be fish nature. But I do stand and sit, I talk and eat solid food, and do other things like those of my species because I have human nature. My human nature also refers to how I think, as well as to decisions I make.

But I am more than just that. There is something special, something *sacred* about me that makes me more than just my human nature. There is an essence to me that makes me unique, unlike anything else in all creation. It is a special quality that makes up my identity as a *person*. It sets me apart from the rest of creation, but finds its expression in my *nature*. So that is how I am a human *person* with a human *nature*. They can't be separated; they make me who I am.

God also has a *person* and a *nature*, but God is not like us. We are made in his image, but images are usually lesser versions of the real thing. Though we have one person and one nature, God is three divine persons with one divine nature.

God has *three* separate, individual essences. They are each unique and unlike anything else in all creation. He has revealed them to us in the simplest of ways: the Father, the Son, and the Holy Spirit. This was revealed to us by the Second Person of the Trinity, who became human for our salvation. Though the humanity of Jesus was born two thousand years ago, the *person* always existed. In fact, in Jesus we see the miracle of one divine person that shared his divine nature with his human nature (one person, two natures, for those of you keeping score at home).

Because the three *persons* share in the same *nature*, we rightly say that God is one. There is no division in him. Though I have human nature and you have human nature, it doesn't mean that we *share* the same human nature. Though we may be similar, you and I think and act differently. But God is of one nature. That is why we don't refer to him as "them." It wouldn't be accurate. God is one. There is no other God but him.

I know you can understand this because God gives you the grace to. Yet though we can get the basic idea, we can never fully comprehend it. This is what the church refers to as mystery. That doesn't mean it's something we'll never figure out, like who killed Jimmy Hoffa or how the pyramids were formed. It's more like diving into a bottomless sea. We can understand the area into which we jump, but we can never reach the bottom of it.

God always was, always is, and always will be. Though revealed

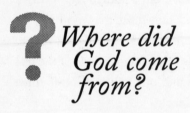 *Where did God come from?*

as Father, Son, and Spirit, the persons of the Trinity didn't "make" each other, nor have they ever been separate. Where did God come from? Good question. To the best of our understanding, God didn't come from anywhere.

He always was. Some try to figure out a scientific beginning to the universe, but nowhere do we see that *something* comes from *nothing*.

Even if you reduce it to sub-atomic particles that existed eons ago, you still have to admit that there was something that wasn't created that created us. That something, or should I say *someone*, is God.

We know these things about God because he has told us about himself. He wants us to know who he is, just like we would be eager to share things about our life on a first date with someone we were attracted to. Learning about the Trinity isn't like learning some kind of trivia. To learn about the person and nature of God is to discover essential information about him whom we are learning to love. And reflecting on these aspects of God's life gives us deeper insight into his love for us, and our identity as lovers of him.

First, the reality of the Trinity tells us that God is never lonely. He did not create humanity out of boredom, but of love. *Real* love. He has no need for our praises, our works, or our affection. His love is completely pure, with no strings attached. And since we were made in his image, we find that we were made to not only love, but to be loved. It is in those moments we feel most complete. Since God is community, we find that we were made for community as well.

As followers of the Trinity, we have the Holy Spirit who dwells in us and brings us to the Father through the Son. The Father is the fisherman, the Son is the rod and reel, and the Spirit is the hook that pierces our soul. He is drawing us into his life. He calls us out of the water and brings us into new life, and this is what we celebrate in the sacrament of baptism. He matures those baptismal graces in us, and this is what we celebrate in confirmation. We can participate in the divine nature, and this is what we do when we receive the sacrament of the most holy Eucharist.

All of our sacraments are encounters with and participation in the life of God. They are moments where we experience heaven on earth, because they place us in the kind of communion with God that we will enjoy permanently in paradise. But notice how all sacraments are celebrated: in *community*. We need each other.

The Community of Saints

So what happens when we die? Do we go on permanent vacation and forget about earth? No. The love that burns in the heart of God burns also in those who love him. God is passionate about saving the lost; don't you think the saints are as well?

By *saints* I mean those who are with God in heaven. They are living their life in eternal community in the presence of infinite love. Words cannot describe the joy they experience, but it's not like they've checked out of reality. Being in the presence of Truth, they *are* reality. They are aware of the battle that goes on for our souls, because they were saved by Christ as well. In fact, the saints in heaven are sometimes called "The Church Triumphant." They're the ones who are with God forever.

Erase the stained glass window stereotype that you have of saints. They're not all dressed in medieval garb. They're from every time, every race, and every culture. And here's something beautiful about them: every one is *unique*. That's right. They aren't cookie-cutter replicas of each other. They are individual, beautiful, radiant souls who get to bask in the glory of God with their brothers and sisters in Christ.

Since God is infinite, he has no problem creating infinitely different people. You don't lose your identity by following Christ, *you gain it*. Paul tells us that, "I am quite confident that the One who began a good work in you will go on completing it" (Phil 1:6). He's the master artist; you are the "work of art" (Eph 2:10). The devil often tries to scare people away from holiness by making them think that Christians are supposed to look alike, talk alike, act alike, and think alike. But what does the world want you to do? Drink the same beer, do the same drugs, listen to the same music, wear the same kind of clothes. Too many people in this world believe the lie that to be an individual, you have to be just like everybody else.

Read about a few lives of the saints to discover that Christians, rather than being conformists, are all so unique! Yes, the saints had the same zeal for holiness, but their personalities, spiritual lives, sense of mission, and even sense of humor varied from person to person. Sin dulls our uniqueness, but Jesus enhances it. He made us, after all.

Let me explain the difference between *saints* and *Saints*. The word *saints* refers to all those in heaven, while the word *Saints* (notice the capital "S") refers to specific people the church declares with certainty are in the eternal presence of God. (How does the church know? It is guided by the Holy Spirit and does in-depth study of that holy person's life.)

St. Francis lived in the town of Assisi, Italy, and gave up everything he owned to follow God. He gathered many followers, and started his own religious order dedicated to preaching the gospel. The Franciscans, as his followers are known, converted thousands upon thousands, and years after his death, the church proclaimed Francis a Saint. My grandmother grew up in East Orange, New Jersey and was a devout Catholic. She taught religious education to hundreds of children at her parish, and raised four children of her own. Up to her death, God was the most important thing in her life, and now she is a saint.

One is a Saint, the other is a saint. The difference? Not everyone in the kingdom of heaven has a public role to play after they've left earth. With Saints, it becomes clear that God is still using the life of this person even after his or her death. The Church studies the person's life in depth, and looks for miracles to demonstrate that the potential Saint is in heaven. After lots of prayer and study, the Church declares that this specific individual lived a life of such holiness that God is lifting the person up as an example for all of us struggling to be holy on earth.

? *Why pray to Saints?*

Many know of St. Francis. Most won't know about my grandmother. That's OK; I ask both of them to pray for me. My grandmother doesn't have to be canonized for me to believe she's in heaven, it just means that God hasn't chosen her for a larger ministry. But I believe she *is* in heaven, like many of my relatives are.

She still cares for me, and *prays* for me. And that's what saints do. They pray for us. They don't have magic powers. They just intercede before the throne of God. James tells us that "the heartfelt prayers of someone upright works very powerfully" (Jas 5:16). That makes sense to us. We would naturally give a prayer request to someone living a holy life rather than to someone who struggled with deep sin. And we would be even more inclined to ask for prayers from someone who had overcome the very thing we were praying for.

? *Why do Catholics seem so fixated on Mary?*

That's why the Church gives us patron saints. They are people whose lives relate to the very thing we are praying for. Remember, you don't lose your individuality when you get to heaven. St. John Bosco spent his life trying to evangelize youth in the late 1800s. He is now the patron saint of youth workers, because that passion in his heart didn't change once he got to heaven. I ask for his prayers a lot.

You should learn about Saints because you will, by God's grace, meet them someday. And you are called to be a saint yourself. Who knows? Maybe he'll even want you to have a capital "S."

But most important, you should ask for saints' prayers. What are you passionate about? Find out the patron saint of that interest and ask him or her to start praying for you. Is there a Saint with your name? Seek his or her intercession.

The queen of all Saints is Jesus' mother, Mary. She has the most intimate relationship with the Holy Trinity possible: she is daughter to the Father, mother to the Son, and spouse of the Holy Spirit. Her beauty is that she is *human* and that God would honor her in such a way. By honoring her, he honors all of humanity. That's why we love her so much. That's why she is our model for faith. That's why we ask for her prayers so often.

But though many things can be answered through Mary's intercession, they are not answered by Mary herself. It is the same with all Saints. We can kneel in our bedroom and in spirit be surrounded by deceased loved ones and famous Saints, and with them all present our request to God. God seems to like it when we get other people involved. And we can do it even when we're praying by ourselves. You don't have to wait until you get to heaven. You can be part of the community right now.

A Word About Angels

God is three divine persons with one divine nature. We each are one human person with one human nature. Angels are one angelic person with one angelic nature. They are different from us. Contrary to some popular fiction, we do not become angels when we get to heaven. They were created in eternity with the freedom to choose God. They serve God, and it is his will they serve us, and protect us from the evil one. Ask for their prayers and protection, because they're always watching out for you!

The Community of Sinners

Doesn't community sound great? I mean, we can participate in the life of God and of the saints! Who wouldn't want to be a part of that? Of course, that's all well and good until it gets down to dealing with people on this planet who haven't been completely purified of their sin and don't dwell in the eternal glory of God. I'm talking about the *jerk*.

You know the jerk. That person who gets under your skin, says bad things about you, and for some reason makes the muscles in your shoulder tense up as he or she walks by. The jerk might even be part of your youth group, and makes you think twice about going to the meeting tonight. Sometimes, the jerk goes on retreat with us, and even stands up to make a decision to follow Christ. We hug him or forgive her and pray that things will be different between us. They do change a bit, because now that person is a Christian.

A Christian *jerk*.

Sad to say, though our eternal state with God can be healed in an instant, our personalities are a bit slower to change. Don't judge too harshly, because maybe it's taking a little longer for God to smooth the rough edges out of *your* life, too. The truth is that these "jerks" can often bring us to greater holiness than we realize. We hate most in others what we hate most in ourselves. When we see the very traits in others we are trying to suppress in ourselves, we often react with great emotion. That's not the other person's fault, it's ours. And God loves them as much as he loves us, even with their (and our) faults. Jesus said, "For if you love those who love you, what reward will you get? Do not even the

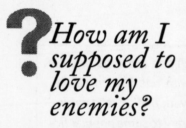

How am I supposed to love my enemies?

[sinners] do as much? And if you save your greetings for your brothers, are you doing anything exceptional? Do not even the gentiles do as much? You must therefore be perfect, just as your heavenly Father is perfect" (Mt 5:46-48).

But be clear on what love is. It's not an emotion, it's a decision. When Jesus says, "love your enemies," he's not asking that we have warm fuzzy feelings toward those who do us harm. He is challenging us to recognize that in spite of our emotions, we should choose to sacrifice for them. That's what he did for us on the cross. Do you think he felt like loving those who were taunting him and spitting at him?

Look, I know it can be hard, but you're part of a family now, and you can't always choose who your brothers and sisters are. And in humility you should realize that you're not so perfect yourself, you know.

There are four reasons you should be an active part of your earthly community:

First, it makes him present. Jesus said that he is where "two or three meet in my name" (Mt 18:20). Jesus is more evident to others the more his followers are together.

Second, it makes us holy. The Letter to the Hebrews says: "With so many witnesses in a great cloud all around us, we too, then, should throw off everything that weighs us down and the sin that clings so closely" (Heb 12:1). It is through community that we learn to be holy. Being in a community with other brothers and sisters in Christ makes it easier to throw off sin. They can keep us accountable for what we do, which is hard but leads to holiness. And it is through community that we can receive the sacraments, which are the most intimate experiences of God's grace that we can receive on this earth. Community fills a need in our souls: we can be loved by those we care about, and we can love those we normally wouldn't.

Third, community gives us perseverance. Hear what Paul writes: "Do not absent yourself from your own assemblies, as some do, but encourage each other; the more so as you see the Day drawing near" (Heb 10:25). It's hard to follow Jesus in a world so often against him. When we gather together, it encourages us to keep running the race. Our time together gives us hope in knowing that we are not alone, and our prayers for each other help strengthen our relationship with Christ.

Finally, your community needs you. Community encourages you to run the race, but your presence in community also encourages others. And hear what Jesus says about the power of community: "May they all be one ... so that the world may believe it was you who sent me" (Jn 17:21). People who gather in his name give witness to Jesus Christ. Even if for some reason you don't feel that you get anything out of community, your presence there is a huge help not only to those who are trying to follow Jesus, but also serves as a witness, reaching out to those who don't know God's love.

Community gives delight to God, purifies and strengthens you, and reaches out to others with the gospel. Don't approach it selfishly. Yes, you need it, but it also needs you. You are not an only child.

Some of you might be in situations where you don't have a community to be a part of, or the one you have isn't very active. Do your best. God knows your situation, and he'll give you grace to make up for what is lacking. Others might have a community, but might not like it and so don't get involved. Well, how is it supposed to change if you're not a part of it? When you serve the body of Christ, you serve Jesus himself. We are all one body, like it or not. So "do not absent yourself from your own assemblies, as some do" (Heb 10:25). Show up. Participate. Pray.

A final but important word that applies to a small number of you. Some of you may have been very hurt, or even abused, by your community or people in it. To love our enemies doesn't mean we let them kill us. There are hurts that are involved in being part of a community of fellow sinners, and that is a normal part of life (whether you are Christian or not). But I am not advocating that you stay in relationships where you find yourself abused or sinned against.

Many of you are blessed with great communities of people who love the Lord and love you (even if imperfectly). Don't take them for granted. Over my many years, I've seen many leave the group because they're dating someone, they're mad at someone in the group, or they just say, "I don't get anything out of it anymore." Years later, they often regret that decision or yearn for the fellowship and teaching that the community offered them.

When you find yourself excusing yourself from praying with others because "I don't get anything out of it," ask yourself the question: what can I *give* to it? Christ is present when two or three gather in his name.

We see community in its highest expression in the Mass. At every liturgy, Jesus Christ becomes physically present: body, blood, soul, and divinity. We can adore him on the altar and receive him on our tongue. This experience can happen even if the homily is boring or

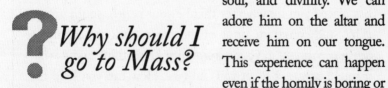

Why should I go to Mass?

the music is bad. Your purpose in going to Mass is to worship the Lord and thank him for his love. You come and give him your prayers, he arrives and gives you himself. What more could you need?

Well, what you *need* is to open your eyes to what is really happening around you. The people who surround you at Mass are really your brothers and sisters. The Scripture read is the Word of God. The "Holy, Holy, Holy" we sing is also being sung with the saints and choirs of angels. The bread and wine become the Body and Blood of Jesus Christ.

Mass is not only the ultimate expression of community, it's the ultimate act of worship we can do in this life. Pay attention to it. Listen to the prayers and the readings. Don't just go to get something, go to *give* something. We are called to do it every Sunday. But would it kill you to also go on a Tuesday?

Whether it be through sinner, saint, or sacrament, God will use community to draw closer to you than you can possibly imagine. Your community prayers will fuel your individual prayers, and vice versa. I know there are lots of obstacles on your path to holiness. But don't worry. God is bigger than all of them.

Just keep running with both feet.

What Should I Do Now?

Make a commitment to whatever spiritual community God has placed you in, whether that be your parish, youth group, Bible study program, or all of the above. Seek to become an *active participant* in your community. Don't think about what it might *take*, ask what you can *give*. How can you help the Church? Go and make a difference.

EIGHT

Hitting the Road

B ut you must do what the Word tells you and not just listen to it and deceive yourselves" (Jas 1:22).

If this book has only taught you to pray quietly in your room, detached from the real world and connected only to others who believe the same things you do, then it has failed miserably. After all, what is the purpose of working out? It is true, that some work out only to look good. Others work out so that they can be healthy and live a longer life. But those reasons are, for the most part, selfish.

Health and fitness are important reasons to work out, but they are not our final goal. You, my friend, are training for war. You need to be strong and healthy to be the most effective in this fight; you are not working out just for the sake of working out. A lifeguard swims with heavy weights not just to look good, but so that she can pull a body to shore. A firefighter climbs up and down a ladder not just to work his heart, but so that he can reach people in time to rescue them. It is the same with you. You pray, you fast, you read Scripture, you go to Mass, you worship with friends, and by doing so you grow strong in Christ. But you're not just doing it to be able to show off your spiritual muscle. You do it so that you can go into the darkness of this world and bring the light of Christ there.

Jesus told us, "You are light for the world.... No one lights a lamp to put it under a tub; they put it on the lamp-stand where it shines for everyone in the house. In the same way your light must shine in people's sight, so that, seeing your good works, they may give praise to your Father in heaven" (Mt 5:14-16). There is a purpose to what we do. There are lives Christ wants to reach, and he wants to use you to reach them.

There are two ways that we bring Christ's light into the world: by reaching out and by speaking up.

Reaching Out

"Then it will be their turn to ask, 'Lord, when did we see you hungry or thirsty, a stranger or lacking clothes, sick or in prison, and did not come to your help?' Then he will answer, 'In truth I tell you, in so far as you neglected to do this to one of the least of these, you neglected to do it to me'" (Mt 25:44-45).

All of humanity is made in the image and likeness of God. That statement is true regardless of gender, race, or even religious belief. When we reach out to serve another, we reach out to serve Jesus Christ, even if that person has never heard his name.

Read the whole story that Jesus tells in the Gospel of Matthew, chapter 25. He makes it quite clear that serving others is not an option but a *mandatory requirement* for his followers. One group of people made it into heaven because they served the lowly. The other group didn't serve, and were separated from him forever. It is important to note that the people in the second group knew him (they called him "Lord"), but their problem was that they didn't recognize him in the poor, the needy, the naked, the imprisoned, and the sick. If we open our eyes, we see Christ all around us ... and he needs our help. How can we say no?

? *How do I start serving others?*

Service starts with awareness and ends with action. Once we allow ourselves to see the face of Christ, our love for him will compel us to reach out and help him in any way we can. Mother Teresa of Calcutta spent her entire life ministering to people in the slums of India. She would pick up bodies lying in the alleys and the gutters, and find a bed for them so that they could die with some dignity. They were often leprous, covered in sores, stained in vomit, and stank of excrement. Once a reporter asked her, of all the disgusting people she had seen in her life, who was the hardest one to minister to? She didn't hesitate with her answer: "The first one. It got easier after that."

There is great wisdom in that statement. The hardest step to take is often the first one. We see that in our natural lives, when as children we often fall as we learn to walk. We can also see that in our spiritual lives, as we try to "walk the walk" of our faith by reaching out to others. At first we may stumble like children, but our heavenly Father holds our hand and helps us to do it.

There are two ways that we can serve others: social action and social justice. I'll use a well-known story to explain the difference. A man was jogging along the river when he heard a child's cry. At first, he kept jogging. *It is someone else's problem,* he thought. But as the cries got louder, he looked and saw the child in the river, gasping for air. The man yelled for help, but others kept jogging, and the child's parents were not around. So he dove in, and pulled the child to shore.

As he got the child to the shore, he heard another cry. Another child was drowning in the river. Without hesitation, he swam to her. But once he reached her, he heard more cries. He looked upstream, and saw numerous children floating down the river.

The man yelled to the people on the shore. Some dove in. Some watched, but did nothing. Some pretended this wasn't happening and kept jogging. One person listened intently to the man's cries, but instead of diving in, turned around and started running upstream.

This made the man furious. "Where do you think you're going? Children are dying here!"

"I know," said the person, "so I'm going to run upstream and see if I can stop it there."

Social action is illustrated by the man in the river helping the children. *Social justice* is illustrated by the man who ran upstream to see if he could put an end to whatever was causing the children to land in the river. Christians are called to put both social action and social justice into practice.

In social action, the child in the river is symbolic of the many people in this world who suffer and are powerless to overcome their situation. Thousands of people die from hunger *every day*. Many are denied basic rights. Others are forced into labor or slavery (yes, it still exists in this world). In some countries, children are forced into the army because they are smaller targets and harder to hit. Families are forced to live in garbage dumps because of their race. People are sent to concentration camps because of what they believe.

There are things that you can do to help these people: collect food, raise money, visit the sick, donate clothing. You are not asked to save the world, you are just called to make a difference wherever you can. Is there a nursing home nearby? Find out which residents never have visitors and go knock on their doors. Is there a soup kitchen downtown? Find out when it serves food, and ask if you can help. If you're not using something, donate it to the poor. Do you really need ten sweaters when people are freezing in the streets?

The hardest step is the first one: that first knock on a nursing home door, that first meal you hand to a homeless person, that first item you donate to someone in need. But you've got to do it. Nobody can do it for you. Don't be overwhelmed. Just make it happen.

Social justice attempts to address the cause of suffering, as illustrated in the person who ran upstream to get to the source of the problem. What is the cause of people's poverty? What is the cause of injustice? Children in other countries are often forced to work fourteen-hour days in horrible conditions, because they provide cheap labor for American companies. Cheap labor means companies can sell their products at a cheaper—more competitive—price here in the U.S. You should let your senators and representatives know that you would rather pay a few more bucks for an item than have an eight-year-old child chained to a table make it more cheaply for you. There are people imprisoned in other countries, and tortured because of their political or religious beliefs. You can write those governments and let them know that you are watching. Many victims have been freed by such letter-writing campaigns.

Social action deals with the symptoms, while social justice deals with the cause. Whenever you try to cure a disease, you have to take care of both things, particularly when the symptoms are so severe that they are fatal. In the United States, we live in a democracy where the government is created by and for the people. So use your voice. Make some noise. Open people's eyes. Change some lives. As a follower of Christ, it's not an option.

As you do it you will feel overwhelmed but also inspired, saddened and yet hopeful, insignificant but also invaluable. The ugliness you might be afraid of will turn into the most beautiful thing you have ever seen. And you will experience God in ways you never have before.

You just have to take that first step.

Speaking Up

"Go, therefore, make disciples of all nations; baptise them in the name of the Father and of the Son and of the Holy Spirit, and teach them to observe all the commands I gave you. And look, I am with you always; yes, to the end of time" (Mt 28:19-20).

We have seen that when St. Francis addressed his followers, he told them, "Go and make disciples of all nations; when necessary, use words." Our actions speak louder than words. But that does not mean that words are unnecessary.

St. Peter tells us, "Simply proclaim the Lord Christ holy in your hearts, and always have your answer ready for people who ask you the reason for the hope that you have" (1 Pt 3:15). When we live the radical life of sacrifice and joy that Jesus calls us to, it will raise some eyebrows. Eventually people will ask, "What's your secret?" That's when you tell them about Jesus.

They don't need to hear a theological exhortation about doctrines of the Church, they just need to hear about how Jesus Christ has changed your life, and how he can change their lives as well. You don't need to be eloquent, you just need to be real.

And you can trust that God will work through what you say. St. Paul, one of the greatest preachers of Christ, wrote, "For I see no reason to be ashamed of the gospel; it is God's power for the salvation of everyone who has faith" (Rom 1:16). Notice how the power lies in the *gospel*, not the presenter. There is no reason to be afraid or ashamed when we talk about Jesus Christ. *He* is the one who will change hearts. We just need to introduce people to him so that he can do it.

? *What if I don't know what to say?*

Talking about Jesus doesn't mean that you have all the answers. It's OK to say, "I don't know that answer, but I'll find out." Preaching Jesus doesn't mean that you have to be perfect. It's an incredible witness to say, "Yes, I've screwed up, but God has forgiven me ... and he can forgive you, too, no matter what you've done." We don't need to be on the defensive with our faith, even if we are being attacked. When we give reasons for our hope, Peter tells us to "give it with courtesy and respect and with a clear conscience, so that those who slander your good behaviour in Christ may be ashamed of their accusations" (1 Pt 3:16).

He goes on to say, "And if it is the will of God that you should suffer, it is better to suffer for doing right than for doing wrong" (1 Pt 3:17). The truth is, there are many that might not like what you have to say. Most are happy to believe in a God who loves them, but a God who wants them to turn from sin and toward him? That's different. There are many who won't want to give up their sinful behavior, even if it's leading to their own destruction. Because God's Word is so contrary to the way they want to live, they may grow angry at the mention of his name.

Don't be afraid of how they may respond. You don't have to convince people to follow God, just share him and what he has done in your life. God is the one who will change hearts. There were people who walked away from Jesus' preaching, so don't think you're going to do a better job and convert everyone you talk to. Just be honest and loving with what you share, and know that God will do his work, often in unseen ways.

When Jesus said to the disciples, "Go, therefore, make disciples of all nations," he was not only giving them a command, but instructing them as well. Let's take a deeper look at that statement, and learn three important principles on how to do it.

Go

The first word Jesus used was, "Go." One definition that Webster's dictionary gives for that word is, "To proceed without delay and often in a thoughtless or reckless manner." There is an urgency to the word. When someone says "go" it usually means "right now." God needs you out there to spread his Word.

To go means that you leave one place and head toward another. Jesus didn't say, "Stay where you are, and make disciples of the people around you." To share the good news of Jesus, it means that we must *go* where Jesus isn't known. Sure, we can tell other Christians how great it is to love the Lord, but how does his kingdom increase by doing that? If Jesus is only known by those who love him, then how will anybody else ever fall in love with him?

Paul makes it clear that "all who call on the name of the Lord will be saved." But he goes on to ask, "How then are they to call on him if they have not come to believe in him? And how can they believe in him if they have never heard of him? And how will they hear of him unless there is a preacher for them? And how will there be preachers if they are not sent?" (Rom 10:13-15). This is why Jesus tells us to *go*. He has sent us to be preachers of his Word. That means we end up in places we would never think, and talk to people we never thought we would, in order to share God's love for the world.

To go also means to get outside of our comfort zone. Some are uncomfortable with sharing their faith for fear they might not be liked, or will possibly offend. But if someone likes you yet doesn't know about God, what good is that relationship? Wouldn't you rather give him a chance to know the lover of his soul, the One who wants to spend eternity with him?

One important thing about this word: God doesn't ask us to go to places where we may be overcome by sin. He is more concerned with us than with us doing ministry to others. Jesus ministered to prostitutes, but he didn't hang out at brothels. We don't want to end up in places where we might fall into sin, or where our presence might be seen as condoning the sinful activity that is going on there.

To go means that we go outside of ourselves, out of our comfort zones, and build relationships with those we might usually not, in order to bring Christ to them.

Make Disciples

The next thing Jesus told us to do was to make disciples. We are not just supposed to be morally good people, encouraging others to be the same. We are to talk about Jesus Christ, and how he died on a cross to set us free from sin.

Too many people see Christianity as just a moral code: don't drink, don't smoke, don't do drugs, don't have sex before marriage. When someone asks, "Why are you saving sex for marriage?" there are two ways to answer that question. One way is to go the moral route: "I think sex is special and want to wait to give it to the person I want to spend my life with." That's a great answer, but notice how nothing was said about God?

Another way to answer that question is like this: "Because God made sex and sex is a holy thing that is supposed to be celebrated in marriage. It's a gift that he wants to give me, and I don't want to ruin it by wasting it with someone I'm not going to spend the rest of my life with." That's the kind of statement that can *make disciples*. Our sharing is not just out to correct sinful behavior, but introduce them to the living God. We let them know that we are the way we are because of his love for us.

It almost seems taboo to talk about our faith with others. One of the greatest tragedies of today's culture is that Jesus Christ is known more as a swear word than as a savior. But you will be surprised at how many people have wondered about Jesus, but never had a chance to talk to someone who knows him. Don't be afraid to say his name and share him with others. If you do it out of love, it won't come across as preachy or pushy. And if you're living the life, people will respect what you have to share.

? *Isn't talking about Jesus like imposing my beliefs on others?*

All Nations

Finally, to whom should we preach? The answer is simple: "All nations." That means *everybody*.

It's hard to understand how radical this statement was for the apostles to hear. At a time when God was seen as a cultural entity, Jesus tells his followers that *everybody* should hear about him. It didn't matter if you were Jewish, Roman, Egyptian, Indian, or African. It didn't matter if you believed in one God, many gods, or no gods. Jesus didn't die for *some*. He died for *all*.

That means that there is no one you can ever know who isn't supposed to hear the gospel. In fact, it's the people who are the farthest away from God that need to hear about him the most. Some people might say they are happy in their lives without God. The problem is, they don't know what incredible love they are missing!

I'm sure people thought radio stories were cool until they saw their first television show. Even if they say no to Jesus, isn't it better that they had a chance to make a choice? We need to share him with *everyone*.

The word Catholic literally means universal. There's a reason for that name. Our church exists in every part of the world and from the highest cathedral to the darkest prison. There are people of every race and nationality in it. (A piece of trivia for those who live in America: did you know that the worldwide Catholic church is only one-third white?) It encompasses every language spoken, and at every moment of the day there is a Catholic church filled with people celebrating God's love for them. Of the estimated six billion people in the world, over a billion of them profess faith in the Catholic Church.

? *What about people who seem happy not knowing God?*

And there's always room for more.

So never write someone off because you think they can't or won't respond to God's message. Some of the world's greatest sinners have turned into the church's greatest Saints. God's message is for everyone, no matter where they're from or who they are.

Live Out Loud

This gift of God that you have received is meant to be shared. This light of Christ that dwells within you is meant to shine. In everything you say and do, people should notice something different about you.

To be truly alive in your faith, you need to reach out and speak up. You're not imposing what you believe on anyone, you're just living out loud. Do great works of mercy, and then tell them who you're trying to be like. Don't be afraid that you'll say the wrong things, just rely on the power of God. *He* is the one who will change hearts. You are just to bear witness to his truth.

It seems like a paradox, but the great secret that Jesus tells us about the joy of living is that life isn't about what you get, but what you *give*. We are not best defined by what we have, but how we love. As a follower of Christ, we must reach out in love to everyone we meet. We need to give food to the hungry, comfort the afflicted, and share the way with the lost. These things aren't optional; they are what Christians do if their faith is real.

You're not working out so that you can look good in the mirror. There are lives to touch and souls to save. God will use every "muscle" you have to break into the world. So grow strong, and stay focused on him. It is amazing to me that we have a God who not only lets us be a part of his kingdom, but also lets us help build it as well. And that's where the real joy of following Christ begins.

But be careful. Once you take that first step, your life will never be the same. You'll never be able to look at the world around you with closed eyes. The reality of what you see will be difficult to bear at times, but at least it will be *real*. As you experience the Holy Spirit working through you, it will become addictive. And before you know it, you will look in the mirror of your soul and find out that you've become more like Jesus Christ.

And isn't that the whole point?

What Should I Do Now?

Let your light shine! You can't help *everyone*, but you can help *someone*. To find whom God wants you to serve, just search your heart. Do you want to feed the hungry? Visit the sick? Work for justice? Whatever desire you have, God is probably the one who put it there. Go with that desire. Take the first step to reach out to someone in need.

Find two people who don't know God's love, and start praying for them each day. Ask God to give you opportunities to share the gospel with them. And when you do, pray to the Holy Spirit for the wisdom and courage to stand for what you believe. Take a moment to write down how Jesus has changed your life, so that when people ask you are more prepared to respond.

Epilogue

When I was two years old, I had a very bad case of pneumonia. So bad, in fact, that I had to be hospitalized and was even put in a "bubble" for a week or two. Doctors have told me that the sickness is probably why, for a long period of time in my life, I had no sense of smell.

The word for people who can't smell is "anosmic," and it's estimated about 4 percent of Americans suffer from such a loss. To be honest, there's not much doctors do about it, at least in my experience. If you lose your sight or hearing, they offer special treatments or even transplants, but if you tell them you lost your sense of smell, they shrug and say, "Well, that's too bad."

I don't blame them. I mean, if you're going to lose one of your five senses it would be my vote for the one to lose. It messes with your taste buds a bit, but it doesn't hold you back as much as losing your sight, hearing, or touch would.

Still, I was handicapped in a way because I couldn't experience as much as others around me. I particularly remember walking into candle shops with my sister. She would love to put the candles up to her nose, and breathe in the aroma of the store. To me, it was just a bunch of colored wax with string sticking out of them. *Don't we have light bulbs these days?* I would think to myself. *What is the point of this store?*

In college I met a neurologist who was much more helpful than my other doctors. He examined me and said that my anosmic nerves weren't dead, they were just inactive. He prescribed some vitamins that he thought might at least help the situation.

They did.

I can't smell as well as others, this I am sure of. But I now can smell *some* things. And one of those scents I can pick up is that of candles. I remember the first time I walked into a candle store and was amazed at all the fragrances there. I went from candle to candle, breathing in everything I could. Suddenly, this store wasn't as stupid as I thought. To this day if I see a candle store, I'll usually pop inside to experience the scents.

The best way I can express that experience is reflecting on what happened to me over fifteen years ago on Colorado soil.

When I gave my life to Jesus, everything changed. It was like I developed a new "sense." I used to walk by candle stores wondering what all the fuss was about. I felt the same way about church. I'd see people kneeling before the tabernacle, and sometimes I would, too. But it didn't mean that much to me. I just knew that other people seemed to get something out of it.

The closer I have grown to Christ, the more my world has changed. Life is completely different to me now that I have experienced Jesus. When I see others, I see the face of Christ. When I go to Mass, I hear the angels singing. When I receive the Eucharist, I'm kissing God. Reading Scripture is like talking to him. Kneeling in prayer is falling into his arms. Sunrises are reminders of his faithfulness, and every moment is another opportunity to grow closer to him.

This is the transformation that Christ will bring in your life, if you continue to focus on him in prayer. I know we've been comparing it to a workout, but don't think that you're the one putting in all the effort. Let him be a part of it with you. And if there are moments where you feel his presence, just stop what you are doing and be still.

I used to think that prayer was something I'd start and then stop, using the sign of the cross as my on/off switch. Now I know that it is something I always do. I used to think that by praying I would get God's attention, but now I know that my time in prayer is just acknowledging that he is always watching, always holding, always loving me. Listen to how he loves us: "Can a woman forget her baby at the breast, feel no pity for the child she has borne? Even if these were to forget, I shall not forget you. Look, I have engraved you on the palms of my hands" (Is 49:15-16).

When he looks at his hand, he does not see the mark left by the nail, but the beauty of our soul. This is the love of God. This love has changed my life, and now nothing will ever be the same.

My prayer for you is this: *let him change you*. As exercising will change the shape of a body into its most glorious form, so will prayer change your life. But though our bodies will fade away, our souls are eternal.

This is the task that is before you, young Christian. This is the prize you seek. Run to win. Train yourself for religion. Let yourself be loved by God.

God will bless your prayers. Just remember: don't do it *for* him, do it *with* him, so that you can become more like him.

God bless you.

What Should I Do Now?

There are five things that I hope this book has encouraged you to do as a young Catholic beginning your walk with Jesus Christ:

1 *I hope you are letting yourself be nourished by God.* You're doing things like reading Scripture every day, actively participating at Mass, listening to Christian music, you've got pictures of him on your wall and in your locker, and you're experiencing sacraments as much as you can.

2 *I hope you are sacrificing time so that you pray every day.* You are using the five forms of prayer as a guideline, and you are making the effort to know him more deeply in your life.

3 *I hope you do the things that will keep you healthy.* You check your conscience every night and try to live a life that would please God. You let Jesus pick you up every time you fall. You ask for forgiveness and forgive others. You receive reconciliation once a month.

4 *I hope you become a part of your faith community.* You actively participate in your church. You join groups in your parish or area that are meant for you, or that you can help with. You go to Mass every Sunday, and maybe other times as well.

5 *I hope you let your light shine for all to see.* You see the face of Christ in everyone around you. You reach out to the poor, the helpless, and the needy. You are not afraid to let people know how Jesus changed your life. You pray for opportunities to share the gospel with others.

These are the basics, the fundamentals. As time goes on, I hope you'll spend more time in prayer, more time in service, more time in community. This is the foundation of your life in Jesus Christ. Never forget the love that calls you. Never forget the face you seek.

Bonus Workout Materials

Things to help you in your quest for spiritual fitness

Powerful Moves

Repetition is an essential part of working out. Those exercises that we do over and over help us establish a routine. They ensure that we are doing the right thing and exercising our entire body properly. But if we don't take them seriously and apply ourselves to them, they just become a waste of time.

It's the same with these prayers. They can either be very powerful or extremely useless. The goal isn't just to say them, but to mean them with our heart. These words allow us to pray more perfectly, and give us deeper wisdom about what we pray (and what we should be praying).

Don't rush them. Take it slowly. Because they are based on Scripture or church teachings, these "powerful moves" can exercise and nourish our soul at the same time!

Our Father

The first prayer that Jesus taught us to pray.

Our Father, who art in heaven
Hallowed be thy name.
Thy kingdom come, Thy will be done,
On earth as it is in heaven.
Give us this day our daily bread,
And forgive us our trespasses
As we forgive those who trespass against us.
And lead us not into temptation,
But deliver us from evil. Amen.

The Jesus Prayer

The repetition of this simple prayer throughout the day calls upon Christ's power and acknowledges his mercy. This is a great way to exercise all the time!

Jesus Christ, Son of God, have mercy on me, a sinner.

The Glory Be

The Church commonly ends many of her prayers by saying this:

Glory to the Father, and to the Son,
and to the Holy Spirit;
as it was in the beginning, is now,
and will be forever. Amen.

Hail Mary

The first four lines of this prayer are taken directly from Scripture. After honoring our Mother, we then make our request: that she would pray for us now and when we die.

Hail, Mary, full of grace,
The Lord is with you.
Blessed are you among women,
And blessed is the fruit of your womb, Jesus.
Holy Mary, Mother of God,
Pray for us sinners,
Now and at the hour of our death. Amen.

The Memorare

Another great prayer asking the intercession of Mary. It is a bold statement of faith in the powerful intercession that she can do for us.

Remember, O most gracious Virgin Mary, that never was it known that anyone who fled to your protection, implored your help, or sought your intercession, was left unaided. Inspired by this confidence, we fly to you, O Virgin of virgins, our Mother. To you do we come, before you we stand, sinful and sorrowful. O Mother of the Word Incarnate, despise not our petitions, but in your mercy, hear and answer us. Amen.

Hail, Holy Queen

This is how we end the rosary, and it is one of the favorite prayers of the church.

Hail, Holy Queen, Mother of Mercy, our life, our sweetness, and our hope. To you do we cry, poor banished children of Eve; to you do we send up our sighs, mourning and weeping in this valley of tears. Turn then, most gracious advocate, your eyes of mercy toward us, and after this our exile, show unto us the blessed fruit of your womb, Jesus. O clement, O loving, O sweet Virgin Mary.

Pray for us, O holy Mother of God, that we may be made worthy of the promises of Christ. Amen.

Prayer to St. Michael the Archangel

In the Bible, the Book of Revelation shows Michael the Archangel in battle with the devil. Michael is the angel faithful to the Lord, while the devil is the one who rebelled. The beauty of this prayer is that we not only ask for him to help us, but we also get to pray for him, that God may hasten the victory in the battle he fights.

St. Michael the Archangel, defend us in battle. Be our protection against the wickedness and snares of the devil. May God rebuke him, we humbly pray. And do you, O prince of the heavenly hosts, by the power of God, cast into hell Satan, and all the evil spirits, who prowl throughout the world seeking the ruin of souls. Amen.

A Prayer of Daily Offering

Talk about a prayer that covers it all! This is great to say when you wake up in the morning.

O Jesus, through the immaculate heart of Mary, I offer you my prayers, works, joys, and sufferings of this day in union with the Holy Sacrifice of the Mass throughout the world. I offer them for all the intentions of your Sacred Heart: the salvation of souls, reparation for sin, the union of all Christians. I offer them for the intentions of all apostles of prayer, and in particular for those recommended by our Holy Father this month.

A Prayer to our Guardian Angel

Everybody has one. This prayer asks that we might be more open to our guardian angel's protection and guidance throughout the day.

Angel of God, my guardian dear,
To whom God's love commits me here,
Ever this day be at my side,
To light and guard, to rule and guide. Amen.

An Act of Contrition
Traditionally, this is what we say after reconciliation.

My God, I am sorry for my sins with all my heart. In choosing to do wrong and failing to do good, I have sinned against you whom I should love above all things. I firmly intend, with your help, to do penance, to sin no more, and to avoid whatever leads me to sin. Our Savior Jesus Christ suffered and died for us.

In his name, my God, have mercy.

The Apostles' Creed
This is not just a statement of beliefs, but a prayer of faith. It is these beliefs that make us who we are as a church. It is for these words that many shed their blood.

I believe in God, the Father almighty,
   creator of heaven and earth.
I believe in Jesus Christ, his only Son, our Lord,
   who was conceived by the Holy Spirit, born of the Virgin Mary,
   suffered under Pontius Pilate, was crucified, died, and was buried.
He descended to the dead. On the third day he rose again.
He ascended into heaven, and is seated at the right hand of the
   Father.
He will come again in glory to judge the living and the dead.
I believe in the Holy Spirit,
The holy Catholic church,
The communion of saints, the forgiveness of sins,
The resurrection of the body, and life everlasting. Amen.

Spiritual Checkup

St. Paul tells us, "For to be distressed in a way that God approves leads to repentance and then to salvation with no regrets; it is the world's kind of distress that ends in death" (2 Cor 7:10).

The purpose of our guilt is to bring us to life, not continually condemn us to death. When we repent, we have no regrets. It is in this spirit that we can examine our conscience. We don't do it to rub our face in what we did wrong, but to offer up our sorrows in exchange for his mercy. We don't walk away from such an exercise feeling horrible about ourselves, but we rejoice that God has shared the truth with us, and given us his mercy when we lived in lies.

We sin in two ways: omission and commission. *Commission* refers to the things we did that we shouldn't have, while *omission* refers to things we should have done, but didn't.

The first commandment is to love God above all, and to have no other gods than him.

- How do we break that commandment? *A different god doesn't have to be something out of Greek mythology. A god is something in our lives that we worship, that we serve, that we hope in for our well-being. Is money your god? Is popularity your god? Is your girl-friend or boyfriend your god? What do you trust in more than God? What do you think about more than God?*

- How do we live that commandment? *What do we do in our lives to show that God is the center of it? How do we treat others? Do we go to church? Do we pray?*

The second commandment is to not abuse the name of God.

- How do we break that commandment? *It's incredible to think that God gave us his name, Jesus. We can call on the creator of the universe by his first name, but we need to use a title for most of the teachers at our school. But how do we use that gift? Do we make it a swear word?*

- How do we live that commandment? *Do we talk about Jesus? When somebody is down, can we say that we will pray to God for him or her? When something good happens, can we say, "Thank you, God" and mean it? Those are ways we can use God's name: for preaching and for praying.*

The third commandment is to keep the Sabbath day holy.

- How do we break that commandment? *If it weren't for the Jewish Sabbath being on Saturday and the Christian Sabbath being on Sunday, then we would not have weekends off. You'd be going to school seven days a week (in many countries where there are no Judeo-Christian roots, that is what happens). The Sabbath is to be a day of rest and worship. Do we treat it like another day of the week? Do we go to church? Do we work unnecessarily?*

- How do we live that commandment? *Go to church! Spend some special time in prayer! Read a bit of the Bible! Take a day off! Get your homework done on Saturday so you can rest on Sunday!*

The fourth commandment is to honor our parents.

- How do we break that commandment? *To honor means more than just to obey. Do we talk badly about our parents? Do we make fun of them? Do we disrespect them? Do we lie to them, use them, or do things we know would hurt them? Instead of treating them as the instruments God used to bring us to life, do we treat them as a means to our own end?*

- How do we live that commandment? *What can we do to honor them? Can we tell them we love them? Can we write them a thank-you note for our life? Can we do something that would help them out? Can we be home when we're supposed to, and obey all their other rules? Trust me, if your parents think that you honor them, you will find a lot more freedom in your house.*

The fifth commandment is to not murder.

- How do we break that commandment? *Jesus said, if you call someone a fool, you kill them with your tongue. Do we gossip? Do we bad-mouth others? Do we kill people's reputations? Do we engage in violence? When someone says they are thinking about having an abortion, do we counsel against it?*

- How do we live that commandment? *Can we say a kind word that can make someone's day? Can we lift up a friend rather than tear him or her down? When we see someone do good, are we as eager to let people know about it as we can be when we see him or her do bad? Can we preach peace? Can we protect life? Can we get involved in pro-life movements?*

The sixth commandment is to not commit adultery.

- How do we break that commandment? *Jesus said that if you look at someone lustfully, you commit adultery with him or her in your heart. Are we watching TV shows or movies that glorify this sin? Do we treat each other as sexual objects? Are we engaging in sexual relationships with others? Are we treating ourselves with purity (and not masturbating or looking at pornography)?*

- How do we live that commandment? *Do we respect others for who they are and not what they look like? Do we refuse to support TV shows, websites, movies, and so forth that thrive on this sin? Can we be proud and vocal in choosing chastity? (There are certainly enough vocal people who don't.)*

The seventh commandment is to not steal.

- How do we break that commandment? *Have we taken what is not ours? Have we stolen something we haven't paid for? Do we pirate music, movies, or software, and make the excuse that everybody else is doing it? Do we have more than we need? Are we wasteful with what we have? Do we waste water and energy, and take it from someone who may need it more?*

- How do we live that commandment? *In the Catechism, the church says that countries that have an abundance of something (like food) should share with others—otherwise it is like they are stealing from them, because God provided enough for everyone in the world. Can you support a hungry child in a foreign country? Can you give the clothes that you don't wear to the Salvation Army?*

The eighth commandment is to not bear false witness.

- How do we break that commandment? *To bear false witness is more than just lying. When we cheat on a test, we claim we knew the answers when we actually did not. Do we cheat? Do we lie? Do we talk one way, but behave another?*

- How do we live that commandment? *Can we be people that say what they mean and mean what they say? Could we live our lives so that our word is our bond? Can we have enough integrity that if we say we'll do something, we'll do it? Can we admit our short-comings?*

The ninth and tenth commandments are to not covet others' spouses or things.

- How do we break those commandments? *Do we envy other people? Are we jealous of other people's accomplishments? Do we do things to ruin people we are jealous of (make fun of them, spread lies about them, not help them when we can)? Do we look lustfully or act lustfully toward someone who is married? (Looking lustfully at single persons is an offense to God and them. Looking lustfully at married persons is not just an offense to God and them, but to their spouse and their family. This goes for celebrities who are married as well.)*

- How do we live those commandments? *Can we be happy with what we have? Can we not judge ourselves by the person next to us? Can we be thankful for the incredible gifts that God has given us?*

Two Kinds of Sin

Scripture tells us there are two kinds of sin (see 1 Jn 5:16-17). One is called *venial*, which means "light," while the other can be *mortal*, which means "death." All sin is serious, but some sins can sever our relationship with God.

A mortal sin would be like me deciding I don't want to be married this week, so I put my wedding ring in my pocket and cheat on my wife. It would break our relationship, and I could not return to that relationship unless I seriously repented. In our spiritual life, that's what the sacrament of reconciliation is for.

The church doesn't have a list of mortal sins, but tells us about the attitudes in our heart that make them so fatal.

First, the action has *grave matter*. That means it's seriously wrong. To steal a dollar from me is not seriously wrong, but to steal one from a homeless person is.

Second, you have *sufficient knowledge* that what you are doing is wrong. That also implies that you are seeking God's wisdom for your actions: you can't avoid learning the truth so that you can say a sinful act is not your fault.

Third, you sinned with *full consent of the will*. That means no one put a gun to your head and made you do it. It also means you were not acting under the impulse of addictions you can't control.

So, an action is mortally sinful when it's very wrong to do, you know it's very wrong to do, and you choose to do it anyway. That kind of action breaks our relationship with God, and we need to receive the sacrament of reconciliation to restore it. You can check out the *Catechism of the Catholic Church* for more of what it teaches on this matter (sections 1852–1864).

The Ultimate Fat-Burning Exercise

Reconciliation is something that can be scary at first, but it gets easier as you go along. "What will the priest think of me?" "What if he yells at me?" "What if he tells my parents?" Those are all questions that race through our minds as we think about going to confession.

Put your fears to rest. A priest hears so many confessions that he doesn't keep track of what he has heard. And don't think that your sins are so unique that they will stand out for him. After all, there are only Ten Commandments to break. A priest is there, not to condemn you, but to show you God's mercy. That's what the sacrament is all about.

The vow of silence that priests take in hearing confessions is one of the most sacred. They *never* reveal what they have heard in the sacrament. Priests have gone to jail for refusing to say what they heard. What happens in the sacrament is between you and God, through the person of the priest. It is like when you receive the Eucharist: it is an intimate moment between you and Jesus, made possible through the presence of the priest.

Sacraments are the way God sheds his grace on us. He created the church to be a dispenser of sacramental grace. Reconciliation is a sacrament of healing when we have wounded our relationship with God (and ourselves) with sin. It can heal the most serious wound, even if we have severed our relationship with God completely. Reconciliation brings us back to the waters of our baptism, to be perfect and without blemish in God's sight. What a gift!

Maybe you haven't gone to reconciliation in awhile, and maybe you've forgotten how. Here's a refresher course, with some useful tips thrown in:

Examine Your Soul

The sacrament starts *before* you get into the confessional. You need to spend time before the Lord, asking him to reveal to you areas of sin in your life that you need his mercy for. Usually we are very aware of one or two sins, but reflecting on the Ten Commandments can help expose other sinful areas of our lives. The idea behind reconciliation is to be *completely* reconciled with God, so it is best when we examine our conscience thoroughly so that we can make a good confession.

There's an examination of conscience (called "Spiritual Check-up") in this book that you can use to help better prepare your soul for the sacrament. Take some moments to pray over that so that you can be freed from the subtle things that hold us back from receiving all the love God has for us.

The Wait

Usually, there is a wait to receive the sacrament. Don't use that as a time to tap your feet or wonder how long it's going to be. *Pray.* Ask God for the grace and courage to help you make a good confession, and pray for others who are in line to receive the sacrament. There are probably other people more scared than you.

Which Priest?

Often there are different priests to choose from. It is perfectly acceptable to wait for one or the other if you want to. This isn't like a fast-food place; you don't have to jump to the first available register. If there is a priest that you want to hear your confession, and another one opens up, just tell the person behind you that they can go ahead.

All priests have the same sacramental power for forgiveness, but you might feel comfortable with a specific priest that you know (or don't know). You don't have to go to your parish priest. I know there are many who (especially if they haven't gone in awhile) would rather confess their sins to a priest that they don't know and will most likely not see again. That's OK for your first few times, but it would be good to get over that fear. You don't want to put yourself in a situation where you wouldn't go to reconciliation just because you're afraid of who might hear your confession.

Traditional or Face-to-Face?

Depending on how your confessional is set up, you usually have two options. You can choose the traditional option, which is confessing behind a screen, or you can confess face-to-face. Both are valid; one is not better than the other. It's all about what makes you feel most comfortable. If the sacrament is being celebrated in a place where they don't have confessionals, then a priest will often have two chairs by him, one in front and one in back. You can sit in which- ever one you like.

The Beginning

Often, the priest will begin by giving you a blessing, to which you respond, "Amen." Then you say, "*Bless me, father, I have sinned. It has been (how long) since my last confession.*" What you are doing is let- ting the priest know when your last confession was. This helps him in ministering to you. Doctors always ask their patients when they last saw a doctor. It helps them to understand what's been going on in your life, and how to best help you.

The Confession

Right after that you can begin confessing your sins. If you're feeling nervous, you can tell the priest that. Try to forget that he's there, and just open your heart to God, telling him all the things you are sorry for. It is a great release to confess our sins. Just get it all off of your chest. You are in a sacred place in a sacred moment that nobody else will ever hear. Just let it go.

It's important that you confess all your sins, especially the serious ones. That doesn't mean that you keep a list in your pocket every time you sin, but it does mean that you don't willingly hold something back. You are healing your relationship with God. Think of it this way: if I pushed my wife in the mud, then threw her into a lake, those would be very serious sins against our relationship. If I came to her and said, "Honey, I'm so sorry for throwing you into the mud," but didn't mention the lake incident, would I be reconciled to her? No way.

In the same way, when we hold back sins we don't get forgiven. You can fool the priest, but you can't fool God. Don't think of it like, "I'll get forgiven of some things, but I'll save others for later." God sees you as a whole person. You are either forgiven or not.

"But what if I forget something?" That's OK. Don't go running back. If you meant to confess it, consider it forgiven. But you are responsible to examine your conscience beforehand. If you don't think about what you are going to confess and because of that you forget something, then that may be another story. That's why it is so important that you spend time in prayer *before* receiving the sacrament.

We confess sins that we do not want to ever do again. If we have the *full intention* of doing that sin again, then it means we are not sorry for it. If I apologized for throwing my wife in the lake, but was planning to do it again tomorrow, that means that I'm not truly sorry! If you have had sex with someone, and have full intention of having sex again, does that mean that you are really sorry for having done it? Now, the reality is that we will sin again, maybe in the exact same way. That's not what I am talking about. When we confess our sins, we are saying that we are sorry for what we have done and we ask for the grace to never sin again. We tell God that we are going to change with his grace. And when we fall again, the sacrament is always waiting for us.

Congratulations! The hard part is done! Now you are ready to receive God's love in an awesome way!

The Penance

Often priests will give you some guidance in what you have confessed. This is a time for him to share some church teachings, advice, or Scripture with you. You can ask questions, or chat with him about it. Then he will give you a penance.

Penance is an action that we do to show God our sorrow. It doesn't make up for what we have done, but it shows that we are sincere. For example, if I have had a fight with my wife, I would bring her flowers. The flowers don't make up for what I may have said or done, but they are a small way to show that I care and that I am truly sorry for what happened. In the same way, our acts of penance are our flowers to God. We may say some Our Fathers or Hail Marys, or just reflect upon certain things. Sometimes priests will say that our act of confession was penance enough. Others might have us do some kind of service. It all depends on the priest.

The Act of Contrition

Then the priest will ask you to make a good act of contrition. You can use the traditional church prayer (which is in the "Powerful Moves" section), or you can say your own. What we do in the act of contrition is that we say that we are sorry for offending God, not only because he doesn't deserve it, but because it destroys our relationship with him. We then pledge to do our penance, avoid sin, and avoid the near occasion of sin (which means we promise to avoid situations that would lead us into sin). Whatever you say, say it from your heart.

The Absolution

Then comes the grace! The priest will say the words:

"God, the Father of mercies, through the death and resurrection of his Son has reconciled the world to himself and sent the Holy Spirit among us for the forgiveness of sins; through the ministry of the church may God give you pardon and peace," and then come the words that make the sacrament effective: "*and I absolve you from your sins in the name of the Father, and of the Son, and of the Holy Spirit.*"

To *absolve* means to *take away*. God has just completely taken away your sins! You respond by making the sign of the cross and saying, "Amen." And you have been reconciled to God!!! Alleluia!!!

The Ending

Make sure to spend time in prayer after you have received the sacrament. Thank God for his mercy. *Know* that you have been forgiven. You have heard the words yourself. You don't need to do your penance immediately, but you should do it as soon as you can. And rejoice! You have returned to the waters of your baptism. Plan on going to reconciliation once a month, or more often if you commit serious sin.

Muscles of Steel

If prayer is a weapon, then the rosary is a nuclear bomb. The rosary brings powerful intercession to what we pray for, as well as a deepening of the mysteries of Christ in our hearts.

Rosary beads help us to pray. To pray the rosary, we:

1) Say the Apostles' Creed (the cross)
2) Say an Our Father for the Holy Father's intentions (large bead)
3) Say three Hail Marys for an increase of faith, hope, and love (three small beads)
4) Say a Glory Be (space before the next large bead).

Now you are ready to enter into the *mysteries* of the rosary (see below). This is where the power of the rosary comes in. The rosary is not meant to be idle repetition of recited prayers, but a deeper insight of the mysteries of Christ through the constant intercession of Mary. THIS IS WHY WE PRAY IT!

Each decade (set of ten beads) is a different mystery. To pray each decade, you pray an **Our Father** (large bead), ten **Hail Marys** (small beads), and conclude with a **Glory Be** and the **Fatima Prayer**, which goes like this:

Oh my Jesus, forgive us our sins, save us from the fires of hell. Lead all souls to heaven, especially those in most need of thy mercy.

At the end of the fifth decade, pray the **Hail, Holy Queen**. (All those prayers are found in the "Powerful Moves" section of this book.)

The Mysteries of the Rosary

These aren't like unsolved mysteries; they are pictures of God's love so powerful that we can never grasp their full meaning. By meditating upon them, we grow deeper into the love of Christ. There are four sets of mysteries we celebrate together as a church family. If you don't know what the mystery is about, check out the Scripture by each of them:

The Joyful Mysteries (Mondays, Saturdays)
    The Annunciation (Luke 1:26-38)
    The Visitation (Luke 1:39-45)
    The Birth of Christ (Luke 2:1-21)
    The Presentation (Luke 2:22-38)
    The Finding of Jesus in the Temple (Luke 2:41-52)

The Luminous Mysteries (Thursdays)
    The Baptism in the Jordan (Matthew 3:13-17)
    First Miracle at Cana (John 2:1-12)
    Proclamation of the Kingdom of God (Mark 1:15)
    The Transfiguration (Luke 9:28-36)
    The Institution of the Eucharist (Matthew 26:26-29)

The Sorrowful Mysteries (Tuesdays, Fridays)
    The Agony in the Garden (Luke 22:39-46)
    The Scourging at the Pillar (John 19:1)
    The Crowning of Thorns (John 19:2-3)
    The Carrying of the Cross (Luke 23:26-30)
    The Crucifixion (Luke 23:32-49)

The Glorious Mysteries (Wednesdays, Sundays)
    The Resurrection (John 20:1-18)
    The Ascension of Jesus (Acts 1:6-11)
    The Coming of the Holy Spirit (Acts 2:1-42)
    The Assumption of the Blessed Mother (When Mary was called into heaven. We get this from the church's tradition, but Luke 1:46-55 is a nice foreshadowing of it.)
    The Crowning of Mary in Heaven (Revelation 12:1-6)